SCROLL ZOMBIES

How Social Media Addiction Controls our Lives

SVEN ROLLENHAGEN

Translated by Karin Shearman

e.

EHRLIN PUBLISHING

Scrollzombies – How Social Media Addiction Controls our Lives

Original title: Scrollzombies – hur beroendet av sociala medier styr våra liv
Translated to English by Karin Shearman

© 2019 Sven Rollenhagen and Ehrlin Publishing
Cover and design: Johan Leijon
Illustrations: Shutterstock
Ehrlin Publishing AB, Jonkoping, Sweden
www.ehrlinpublishing.com
ISBN 978-91-88375-90-2

"The mobile phone has become the remote control for our lives."

Anna Wikland, Head of Google Sweden

CONTENT

1. Introduction

Almost everyone does it. Presidents and common citizens. Most of the people you know and probably even you. Children and adults on their way to work and school. Whilst waiting for a bus, in the bathroom or in the middle of a meal. We all look down at a screen, scrolling like zombies through the flow of social media. Cat videos, advertisements, sunsets, news, memes and selfies. It all flickers past in a flash. Often we don't even think about what we are doing. It happens automatically as soon as we get the chance.

The mobile zombie is deeply absorbed in its phone. It walks around clutching it in its hand and can bump into someone or walk into a lamppost. I used the term mobile zombie in my previous book about the dos and don'ts of mobile use. The scroll zombie is closely related to the mobile zombie. It appears when you are aimlessly scrolling through your flow on social media. There is no real reason behind your actions – your fingers move automatically on the screen. Sometimes you become completely absorbed by the screen and your surroundings become irrelevant.

Social media takes up a large part of everyday life for most of us. The subject affects all of us and our opinions differ. Many people I have spoken to feel that social media takes up too much time in their lives and interferes with other activities. As an addiction expert, I have had the chance to help these people create a balance in their digital lives. I meet people who take regular detox breaks, but I have also met those who do not care at all about their use of social media. They would rather be left alone from what they see as moral preaching.

I am a social worker and have worked with dependency issues since the eighties. Over the last few years, I have specialized in different types of digital addiction, mainly video games, social media and mobile phones. I have carried out some pioneering work on video game addiction, now a WHO-recognized diagnosis. I have helped many people regain control over their gaming and use of screens. Many of these people now have a functioning life with work, family and, what I choose to call, good digital health.

These days, I see a more mixed type of screen addiction in my patients. Instagram, YouTube and Snapchat are competing with homework and sport. Many of my clients are adults whose work, relationships and spare time are affected by social media.

I, myself, play video games and I am an avid user of social media. I have a positive view on technology and a curious attitude towards all things digital. Throughout most of the time writing this book, I have been active on social media. I have used what is known in sociological research as participant observation. This means that the person studying a phenomenon does not do it from an external perspective but participates in the activity being observed. This has provided me with invaluable information as a compliment to my extensive experience in treating people.

Writing about digital issues is a challenge. This is because, by the time you read this, I expect the availability of platforms and technology for social media will have changed and will look somewhat different. But I am convinced that, even though the shape of addiction can change, there will always be characteristics of dependency that are timeless.

I have previously written books on video game addiction and mobile phone etiquette. Parallels may also be drawn to this type of addiction. In this book, my focus is on our conflicting relationship to social media. I have interviewed researchers, talked to friends and relatives as well as other people I have met in daily life about their views on social media. Additionally, this is a book built upon personal reflections and thoughts.

In this book I shall keep referring to my own life on social media. About how I was engulfed by, above all, Facebook, a realization that I was hooked and about how I broke free. This journey is described at the end of the book under the headline "How I got stuck online and created a digital balance". Maybe you will recognize yourself in my experiences, be inspired to create your own digital balance, or you can choose to see it as a thought-provoking subject.

I see my own use turning into an addiction as a strength. Because I know what I am talking about when the pressure to be active online feels like a compulsion. But today I have come out of my addiction and formed a healthier relationship with my digital life.

I deliver this book from three different perspectives. That of the addiction expert, that of the person who, himself, has suffered from an addiction, and the third perspective, that of the parent. My children grew up in the middle of the digital revolution and, to begin with, I had no understanding of my children's digital interest. But, together with my own use of social media, I have gained a better understanding and insight into this modern way of socializing. There is, as yet, no clinical diagnosis called social media addiction. The topic is relatively new and uncharted even though there is ongoing research. However, the term social media addiction is already used widely all over the world. It describes the state where people seem to lose control over their use of social media. Since it is a simple and clear term, I will also use it.

My view of social media is pragmatic. I take people's experiences of dependency-causing phenomena seriously, but I believe that social media can be a source of both good and evil. I have existential and holistic values, which means that I believe you yourself have the possibility to shape large parts of your life by the choices you make. What you have for breakfast, whether you smoke or not, whether you exercise or are inactive – and how you choose to live your digital life. I believe body and soul are intimately connected. If you exercise your body, you will feel better psychologically. If you are depressed, your physical health can also suffer. Life is a constant balance between physical and psychological health. In my work, I take an optimistic view on change. Even if you are in a negative dependency, there is always the possibility to stop and initiate a change. The choice is yours.

2. Our lives online

The digital revolution

The digital revolution is an ongoing process. What was previously analogue has become more and more digital; payment solutions, medical technology, entertainment, navigation and communication. More and more platforms are appearing, making possible smooth dialogue between people. This is where social media has an important function to fill.

We spend more and more of our time on social media. Some of the biggest platforms are Facebook, Instagram, Twitter, Snapchat, WhatsApp and YouTube. Here we broadcast our lives, sharing everything from simple day-to-day events to weddings and funerals. Social media is open round the clock, all year round, providing information to more than three billion users across the world.

What social media do you use?
Which ones do you like the best?
Is there any platform that you feel creates problems to you?

The coin has three sides

At the beginning of the digital revolution, the discussions about social media were mainly positive. There was talk of a new and fantastic way of socializing that gained more and more followers. The debate about the downside of social media has not been going on for as long. The first time that I spoke publicly on the subject was in the Swedish national newspaper Aftonbladet in 2009. It was an article about young people's Facebook habits, about how students were becoming hooked on Facebook, ignoring homework, mealtimes and other important activities.

In the last few years, media has increasingly picked up on what is commonly known as social media addiction. The importance of Facebook and other similar platforms in people's lives becomes clear as soon as there is a technical issue. People may despair and show symptoms of withdrawal. I remember once when it happened to me. I was posting something in a group and received an error message. At first, I thought I had poor internet coverage, but the connection was fine. Shortly afterwards I received a message saying that there had been a technical fault affecting Facebook and other platforms. When I asked friends about their reactions, many said that it had stressed them out, which it had me too. The disruption only lasted for a short while, but long enough to make me realize that I had become so used to my feed that it stressed me out when it stopped.

Research into social media is still in its infancy, which is not particularly surprising. The problems are new, and research takes time. A single study is not sufficient. It is only long-term and collective large-scale research that can lead to real and stable conclusions. The internationally renowned researcher, Mark Griffiths, summarizes the current situation well: "There is still a lack of large-scale qualitative studies."

This lack of reliable studies has led to a partly polarized debate in the media. Initially, there were two dominant groups. One group was technology-friendly and focused on lifting the positives of social media. This group took the view that the discussions surrounding the negative effects were no more than a moral panic in response to something new and unknown. Once we became used to it, the worry would diminish, in the same way as we had previously got used to rock music and violence in movies – phenomena which caused concern from the start but which subsided once we realized that it did not turn people into lunatics. Their solution was to embrace the new technology with open arms.

Then there were those people who wanted to paint a darker picture. Their view was that the radiation emitted from mobile phones was deadly and that we would never be able to learn how to handle modern technology. One example was that of someone falling over a cliff because he was staring down at his mobile. This was an extreme

Important milestones for social media

2003. LinkedIn was launched, a network for working professionals and researchers.

2004 marked a great change for many people. Mark Zuckerberg launched Facebook.

WhatsApp was founded in **2009** and can be used for sending text, pictures and films.

2000

2003. Skype launches as a free service for talking and chatting online.

In **2005** YouTube saw the light of day. Being able to share films instantly became a huge success. Being a Youtuber is one of many new digital professions.

Twitter was launched in **2005**. Here you post short messages of up to 280 characters.

case that was presented as something that could happen to anyone, but of course this was not a typical everyday occurrence. This group was in favor of rewinding time to the days of analogue technology.

I can still see one-sided reporting where social media is either raised positively or is one-sidedly criticized, but this is starting to change. More and more people seem to take a more balanced view on these phenomena. Many people, me included, want to bring forward *all* the different sides of digital technology, the positives, negatives and everything in between. This more nuanced group includes everyone from practitioners like me, researchers and users themselves. Doesn't it make sense to be open to the coin not having just one side, but three?

I have spoken to one of the world's leading researchers into social media addiction, Dr. Mark Griffiths. He is a Distinguished Professor of Behavioural Addiction at Nottingham Trent University, England, and is one of the most qualified researchers in the field. He has

In **2010** Instagram was launched, a platform with a focus on pictures.

In **2011** Snapchat was born. A service where pictures and films can be sent between users.

2020

In **2011** Messenger was launched. This meant that we were able to send direct messages to a Facebook friend.

In **2014** Jodel was launched. A challenger to other commercial platforms since it is anonymous and free from advertisements. A Jodel can only be seen within a 10 km radius and other jodellers can up or down vote a post. After five down votes, the Jodel is killed.

conducted studies on gambling, video games and social media.

Griffiths believes that the normal state for the younger generation is to be constantly online. Communication using social media is a given. The young do not want to miss anything. FOMO (Fear of Missing Out) is a term that is highly relevant. A young person wants to be constantly updated via social media. What their friends do, as well as their thoughts and opinions, are important. Griffiths believes that we need to take this into account when we evaluate the use of social media. This is also my own experience; what feels like a dependency to the older generation can be a natural part of life for a younger person.

Griffiths thinks that social media can create problems for *a small minority* of users. It depends on the individual and how they use it. When social media takes focus away from work, studies and other activities, it has gone from being something useable to an addiction maybe *forcing* you to do things you don't really want to do. He emphasizes that, just like video games, social media does not create problems for the vast majority of users.

Most people have complete control. But a small minority experience negative consequences and it is these we need to focus on. We must look at the bigger picture, not just focus on how much or how little time we spend in the digital sphere.

On the other hand, there are studies showing that social media can also have positive effects. It is about what you do and how much. Take these two extremes as an example: zombie scrolling on Instagram or looking for help on a Facebook group when you are depressed. Which one will make you feel better? I normally compare this with the way we eat. If you eat healthy food in the right amounts you will feel great but if you eat junk food in excessive amounts you will become ill. The same thing goes for social media: if used wisely, a digital presence makes us feel good but, if we lose control, it can lead to addiction.

Analogue vs. digital life

Two people are admiring a beautiful sunset. They are on holiday, far away from work and other responsibilities. They are enjoying a calm sea where the sun is slowly setting. One person takes out their mobile, takes a photo and then puts the mobile away. The other person does the same thing but immediately posts the picture on Instagram. While the sun is disappearing, that person is staring on his screen, waiting for likes. When he looks up, the sun is gone. The likes are flooding in and he shows this to his friend who becomes irritated that Instagram became more important than them being together.

Who did the right thing? What do you think?

I see four possible ways to act in this type of situation.

* Enjoy the sunset and don't bother about your mobile
* Take a photo with no intention of posting it
* Take a photo and post it straight away
* Take a photo and post it later

This is a good example showing that we usually have a choice in how we act when it comes to social media. For many of us, these choices are routine. We do not reflect on the alternatives we have, instead it happens quickly and automatically. But if we start making more conscious choices, we can affect how our use makes us feel.

At the beginning of the digital revolution, many people claimed that there was a difference between the so-called real life and our digital life. The term IRL (In Real Life) is based upon the (mis)conception that the digital world is not real. The idea was that the digital sometimes made interactions IRL more difficult and it was better to focus on IRL. Nowadays, I and many others prefer not to use the term IRL, but instead use the term "analogue", in other words, non-digital. This way, we avoid the emotive bias that is associated with IRL.

More and more people seem to want to go back to an analogue way of life. To a life without internet and screens. Or at least to a life where we minimize the use of digital technology. Steve Jobs was extremely restrictive when it came to his children's use of technology. He was sometimes called a "low-tech parent". One of the biggest developers of technology of all time possessed great insight into the negative consequences that the digital world could create.

These days, IT employees have taken Jobs' skeptical stance. But what do "normal" people think about this? I see more and more signs of concern about our digital technology, since social media can diminish social contact between people. That it becomes a wedge that divides, rather than the glue that binds. We can see conflict where people meet, yet are constantly interrupted by someone else making contact digitally. A notification from an app telling you that something has happened, then suddenly there is a mobile in your hand and the current conversation gets cancelled. Or can we talk about an expansion of relations? A modern way of looking at it is to determine that there is no barrier between the analogue and the digital. That we merely flow between different ways of communicating. In the same reality but without conflict. Everything is integrated. Without prejudice about which is best.

I believe it is wise to choose different strategies in how to use digital technology. It does not have to be black and white. We do not need to choose to be hyper-digital and constantly connected, nor do we need to be like Thoreau and build a log cabin in the woods with no modern technology at all. I believe there are active choices to be made in order to create balance.

Have you ever longed to go back to a completely analogue life?
Do you think you could live without social media?
What would the consequences be?

"Men have become the tools of their tools."
David Thoreau, Walden (1854)

User groups

When we discuss social media, often only two groups feature. Those who are digital and those who are analogue, that you either use social media or you don't. I believe it is good to differentiate even more, so I place digital users into four groups. One advantage of talking about different user types is that it is easier for us to understand one another. We are able to accept one another's digital habits and therefore avoid unnecessary conflicts.

1. Digital natives have grown up with digital technology. They have a natural and relaxed relationship with social media. Everything is done quickly and smoothly as though on auto pilot. They use different social platforms as a natural hub for communicating with other people. They rarely see a difference between analogue and digital – their reality combines both, they are just different ways of keeping in touch. Both of my children who were born in the 1990's belong to this group.

2. Digital immigrants have discovered modern technology as adults. They normally have a more skeptical and dubious stance. I, myself, have asked my children: "Wouldn't it be better to go and knock on their door or give them a call?" when they have wanted to chat with friends living next door. I wondered why they couldn't meet properly instead. Which the children thought they already did. But online. Digital immigrants can learn to socialize digitally but it does not always run smoothly. They often ask younger people for help with digital problems. A digital immigrant likes to use the term IRL and divides the world into analogue versus digital reality, where the analogue is seen as better than the digital.

I, myself, am a digital immigrant trying to take in the modern way of socializing. When chatting to my children on Messenger, I can tell my partner that I have "spoken" to them and I often have rewarding meetings with clients via Skype.

3. Digital outcasts are outside of social media. This group can be split into two sub-groups:
- Those who are virtually completely analogue. They use neither computer, mobile nor social media. They read newspapers, pay their bills on paper and use cash. This group contains mainly older people who, for different reasons, have not entered the digital world. The group is often seen as being discriminated against in today's society because there is more and more expectation to be connected. We are starting to talk more and more about a digital alienation. My mother, born in 1927, is a good example of this sub-group.
- The other sub-group is made up of people who use computers, the internet and mobiles but are outside of social media. I have several friends and relatives belonging to this group. Some of these are accused by others of being Facebook freeloaders. They do not want to be active themselves but like to keep abreast of the information through friends and family.

4. Digital emigrants. This is a relatively new phenomenon. It relates to people who are fed up with their digital lives. They experience a digital stress and try to minimize their time online. The choice is then to do a digital detox for a shorter or longer period of time. In the most extreme cases, they can go out into the countryside where they reject all digital technology. I have a relative who sometimes goes out to our shared country house, leaving the computer at home. The mobile is switched off and the focus is on painting and meditation.

The Analouge Author

Ernst Brunner is one of Sweden's most productive authors. We go to the same gym and often share our thoughts about writing, but also about our digital presence since he is completely inactive on social media. He has made a decision to remain on the outside. No Facebook. No Instagram. His digital life is empty. I have never seen a mobile phone in his hand. He communicates mainly by email, but prefers to write physical letters sent by snail mail.

   I have sometimes wondered if it is possible to live by analogue means in the 21st Century and at the same time be a renowned author. Normally, an author has a broad social media network to reach readers, media and the book business. I should also add that, these days, he is less in the spot-light than he was previously, so it may not matter as much to be outside of the digital life. Or does this make him antisocial, avoiding human contact? On the contrary. At the gym he is one of the most sociable people there. He talks to everyone he knows and even complete strangers. When you talk to him, he looks you in the eye and not at the screen of a mobile. As I am not in contact with him via social media, our interaction is different. We only talk when we meet. This means we usually have more to talk about. We have not been able to follow each other's lives on social media.

Sometimes there are clashes between the groups since the frames of reference are different. It is a common occurrence that those who are not active themselves on social media are critical of those who are. I have also encountered the opposite, that those who are active have problems understanding those who have chosen not to be.

I, myself, was skeptical before I became an active user. This was the result of me not fully understanding what was actually going on out there. Standing on the sidelines and watching, is not the same as taking part. When I became active on social media, my view changed radically. I experienced joy, fellowship and felt that my life had new meaning. I understood why people spent a lot of time on social media. It was simply another way of socializing.

What group do you belong to?
Do you see conflicts that can arise between the different groups?
Have you ever thought of changing group?

Digital friendship

No-one can have more than 5,000 friends. At least not according to Facebook. Perhaps you didn't know, but Facebook has a limit that does not allow any more than 5,000 contacts. Most of us realize that the majority of these contacts cannot be "real" friends – people we have met through analogue interaction. There are researchers who believe that we can only handle around 150 relationships. But perhaps it is time to re-evaluate what friends actually are. What about friend-ships made online, are they "real"?

I know several people who I have never met in the analogue world, but I am in regular contact with them via social media and Skype, and I consider them my friends. It is also common that my clients have made friends, via online games, who they have never met in "real" life.

The exciting thing is how even online friends can feel like "real" friends, that the digital relationship can create strong bonds between people. It is comparable to the pen-pals of old. Back then, two people could exchange letters over a long period of time, getting to know one another, even though they had never met. Today, people meet in a similar way online in a simple and natural way.

There is a current discussion where some argue that the old way of socializing is better, that having too much focus on online relationships may bring negative consequences. For example, Professor Fred Nyberg suggests: "Getting stuck behind a screen may result in diminished social skills IRL. This especially concerns young people who, because they experience less physical contact, risk impairing their ability to read body language and mood."

I often meet young people with amazing skills in the digital world, but who, at a social event, have under-developed social competence.

Personally, I believe there should be no opposition. The best thing should be to support both digital and analogue friendships. This way, you reduce your chances of being lonely. I notice this clearly if I am alone and writing. I can then quickly and simply engage in some social interaction via social media. At the same time, I do not see this as any different to meeting someone for a coffee.

Do you have friends who you only meet online?
Do you see any difference in these friendships compared to those friends you meet in person?

The quest for the perfect life

Seeing how other people's lives are portrayed on social media, we risk becoming anxious or even depressed. Our feeds are often dominated by happy occasions – we post pictures from a wedding, an amazing dinner or a beautiful sunset from an exotic location. We rarely share the grey normality, despite it being the greater part of our lives. If we start to compare our own lives with others, who seem perfect, it can cause jealousy and depression.

There are, of course, exceptions. Such as my friend Anders who, every working day, posts a picture from his commuter train as it passes Rotebro – a rather grey and dull commuter station in Sweden. But it is part of his everyday life. I also have several friends who have openly spoken of their divorces and difficult medical conditions. But is there really any difference in how we portray our lives online compared to when we meet in person? Do we tend to focus on our happy times when we meet in the analogue form? Yes, maybe, but I believe that meeting in person makes it easier to discuss all aspects of life. Happiness, illness, grief and joy – just like life itself. But if we examine the feed in our social media, much of the focus is on the positive aspects of life.

Adults are able to understand that what we see on social media is just a selection from a person's life, a façade that does not show everything. But what happens to a young person who is constantly exposed to the "perfect" lives of others?

In the last few years, mental ill-health has risen amongst young people. More and more young people are seeking help for anxiety and depression. Many testify that there is a type of silent competition on social media; we must show gorgeous, well-trained bodies; life must be filled with excitement, success and happiness. This can create a very noticeable form of performance anxiety. I once had a client who was severely affected by this phenomenon. Comparing himself to others caused him to feel so bad that he became suicidal. His solution was to take a step back from social media. In combination with therapy treatment, this made him feel better and better and eventually his suicidal thoughts disappeared.

Does this mean that we would all feel better if we completely distanced ourselves from social media? It need not be so drastic, but I believe it is important to ask ourselves the question of "how" we use it. There is always a choice as to which people I follow and which platforms I use, and how much. In some cases, social media can even help to cure mental ill-health.

There are groups on Facebook that can support you if you are struggling with mental ill-health. I sometimes read posts from people with depression who receive some quick, encouraging support from other people who have been in similar situations. In such groups you are able to get help immediately and without delay. I am in a group myself where we encourage one another if we are not feeling well. It can include simple everyday tips such as taking a walk to seeking emergency help when having suicidal thoughts.

The strength behind getting help through social media is that it is available around the clock, and that you are able to get support immediately. The downside is that it requires a certain ability to be selective with the information given. There is no quality control on social media, when compared to standard healthcare. Therefore, the person administering such groups has a great responsibility, since it can literally mean life or death. I see this type of help as a variation of community support, that should not be seen as professional healthcare but more like the support we might receive from family and friends.

I often meet people who, deep down, suffer from poor self-esteem. These people run a higher risk of feeling low when comparing themselves to "happy status feeds". But it is also about who we choose to follow, because the opposite can also be true: that a person feeling low can be lifted by a fitness profile who encourages physical activity. Exercise is often a simple and effective way of improving your mental well-being.

Digital footprints

When you post a picture, a text or a link, you produce a digital footprint. These can then be seen by anyone, such as an employer. The difference with the time before the internet is that your footprint can remain for a very long time and can even be spread wider online. So, you need to think about the impression you want other people to have of you. It is increasingly common for employers to check potential employees' digital footprint. To optimize your possibility of getting the job, you should pay attention to what you post.

I spoke to a college student about this. She had had an internship work experience at a local restaurant and had later applied for a summer job. She was well-liked during her work experience internship, receiving some good references afterwards. But something unexpected happened during her interview for the summer job. The kitchen manager had made a Google search of her, finding pictures on Instagram showing her and her friends having wild parties. The end result was that, despite her excellent references, she did not get the job since the company was very particular about what their staff exhibited online. When she posted the pictures, she hadn't given any thought to how her digital footprint would affect her in the future. She had to learn this the hard way.

What is your feed like?
Do you get jealous when you see other people's happy lives appear in your feed? Or does another person's success encourage you?

3. Why do we get hooked on social media?

For some time now, we have been suffering a digital hangover. News headlines focus solely on the negative side of modern technology: mental illness, stress and addiction. But in the middle of this we must also remember the other side of the coin, that social media generates a fair amount of positive effects. Otherwise we would hardly spend such an incredible amount of time on these platforms.

Social media fills many functions, but how we use it can be different amongst different people. For me, it is a mixture of things. I can get inspiration and tips for my writing from a Facebook group. Or I can look for suitable hiking routes when going on holiday. Facebook and Google have an answer for almost everything. As long as I question the source, there is a great deal of information available, quickly and simply.

I communicate and socialize with friends, family and colleagues, as well as with strangers. I have realized more and more that friendships can grow online. I know several people who I have only ever had online contact with. Sometimes for the practical reason that we live too far apart, but also because the contact via social media has felt sufficient. Social media shrinks our world and I can communicate with people regardless of where they live.

On social media, I have access to an open stage, where I can air my thoughts, ideas and problems. Social media is always open, and I get a quick response. Sometimes it feels like participating in an enormous digital group therapy session, the difference being that I do not always know who is offering the advice. I have several friends who have spoken openly on social media about serious illness, divorce and financial problems. They normally say that it is good to be able to reach everyone easily through mass messaging, so that they do not need to contact everyone they know separately.

I also use Facebook as a natural way of communicating with my clients. A big difference from previous communication is that social media creates more dialogue. Not just one-way information as you would have found in a newsletter. This can make it difficult to switch off from work, especially if you run your own business, and your online contacts may determine your success.

People have a need to escape reality quickly and simply. Every time I look at a video of a cat, it cheers me up. In only a few seconds, a funny cat clip will make me smile. Social media can deliver everything you wish for. Discussions, funny pictures, beautiful places. It is all there in a never-ending feed. There are no obstacles to reaching all of this. A couple of clicks on your mobile phone is all it takes.

Social media is also used to foster "people empowerment", where a large group of people can gather around an important topic. The #metoo movement is an example of something that would not have taken off, had it not been for social media. Social media is also used in presidential campaigns and elections as a tool to attract voters and influence large numbers of people. Today's leaders now have regularly updated Twitter accounts – for better or worse.

I have also spoken to the Swedish environmental activist, Greta Thunberg, about her work on climate issues. She was convinced that the internet and social media was vital in spreading her message globally. I am sure she is right. I was, myself, active in environmental issues in the 1970s, long before the internet. Back then it was considerably more difficult spreading a message in the old analogue way.

What advantages do you see in using social media?

Fast clicks and kicks

I am not alone in having been hooked on using social media, but what is it that makes it so hard to find a balance in our digital use? In this chapter I will separate which factors are specific to social media because, even though different dependencies can have a common core, every addiction is unique.

Imagine a large bowl of potato chips on a table. You are at a party, mingling with a drink in your hand. You are mixing conversation with drinking and eating chips. Have you ever seen a person satisfied with taking just a single potato chip? I know I haven't. Sometimes I meet people who do not eat any chips at all, but for those of us who sometimes enjoy potato chips, one is usually not enough – we simply want to relive the quick reward. Fat and sugar give immediate small kicks.

Social media works in much the same way. When someone likes my post, I get a buzz. It is about confirmation that somebody else thinks I have done something good, even if I have only posted a picture of a sunset. It gives a feeling of pleasure and I want to repeat that feeling. So, I post a new picture, get a new kick and the wheel is in motion. The fact that it all happens at the speed of light affects how deeply we get hooked. The risk of getting hooked is affected by activities with a quick response. Take, for example, a scratch card and a lottery ticket. A scratch card provides an immediate kick, whilst a lottery ticket makes you wait several days for a result.

Similar phenomena occur when I see pictures on Instagram or a funny video clip. I enjoy it, smile and want to relive the feeling of being entertained. This is often an automatic process – we don't really think, but our fingers are scrolling as if they have a mind of their own. Just like the fingers searching for the bowl of potato chips.

When our brain gets used to all of these small kicks, we may become caught in the typical cycle of click and kick. Taking your mobile to the bathroom is a sign that we have problems in breaking this cycle.

Another important aspect is chance. You never receive exactly the same number of likes for your posts. This triggers your curiosity in checking how it is going, since you do not know from the start if you will get the odd like or an avalanche of likes. It is the same system triggered by scratch cards and other types of gambling. The excitement is created by you not knowing the outcome. Sometimes you win, but not always. If everyone knew the outcome of a game beforehand, gambling would not be as exciting and addictive.

I have spoken to an expert to get his view on this. Fred Nyberg is a professor of biological dependency research at Uppsala University in Sweden and is one of Sweden's most qualified researchers in this field. Nyberg suggests that social media creates powerful kicks via our brains reward mechanism. An increase of dopamine makes us happy, leading to us wanting to experience that feeling again. And again… and again… At this point, a like on Facebook or Instagram can have a similar effect as a glass of wine to an alcoholic. A common expression for this phenomenon is that the brain gets hijacked by an addiction. The individual loses control and the dependency drives the behavior.

The tricky thing with dopamine kicks is that we cannot avoid them when they start. However, we can choose not to expose ourselves to them in the first place. Or at least try to ration them. I sometimes buy a small bag of potato chips, rather than a large one, for exactly this reason.

The like button has been accused of being one reason for people becoming hooked. It is quick and simple to like, and you immediately receive a small kick. Even the creator of the like button, Justin Rosenstein, is seriously worried about the dependency-creating function that he has created. He says that this did not happen by coincidence. It was carefully calculated that people would start clicking, almost manically, on this button. Even previous Google employee, Tristan Harris, confirms that companies use psychology to keep us on the platforms. Both of these people are now engaged in activities aimed and helping people create digital balance; *Time Well Spent* and *The Center for Humane Technology*.

The knowledge of how to hook a user exists within Facebook and other technology companies. Psychologists and behavioral scientists are key people in this work. The way social media is constructed is no coincidence. The companies possess a great deal of knowledge of what triggers us. Here they do the same as all other businesses, they use their knowledge of human behavior in order to maximize their sales. The question is where to draw the line. When does it become unethical to trigger a dependency? We will come back to this important question in the chapter about social responsibility.

Do you experience kicks from social media?
How strong are those kicks?
Do you get similar kicks from other activities?

Humans are social creatures

"We are profoundly social creatures", writes Matthew D. Lieberman, professor of psychology, in the book *Social, Why Our Brains are*

Wired to Connect (2013). Lieberman suggests that humans are basically social creatures. We need social relationships with others in order to feel well. When I walk to my office – a walk that normally takes five minutes – it often takes twice as long. The reason is that I have lived in the area for a long time and know many people that I meet on my way. When I bump into someone, I can stop and chat for a while, about anything from simple day-to-day events to the fear of new terror attacks. These simple social meetings are important to us humans. It becomes a glue that brings us closer to one another. I think this is a major reason for social media having become so popular; we are tempted by the possibility of communicating with others.

Here, as I am sure you suspect, lies a paradox. Humans are social beings who need social relationships to survive. Involuntary loneliness can lead to increased psychological ill-health and people who suffer from loneliness can show signs of depression – a serious illness that can lead to suicide.

Most of us want to belong to groups and be part of something meaningful. Of course, a workplace, a school or a sports club can offer this, but there are those who do not feel as though they fit in anywhere or have problems in leaving the house. In such situations, a kinship via social media can work wonders. I have met autistic children who, thanks to the internet, are finally able to have better social relationships, via gaming or social media.

But on the other hand, we can become hooked on social media turning it into a negative, making us less social in the analogue world. What happens if I stare at my screen whilst taking a walk? Well, I miss out on the day-to-day social interactions. The online contacts on social media push away my other "analogue relationships".

I asked my Facebook friends if social media made them more or less sociable. Most of them felt they became more sociable. They were able to have contact with people they would otherwise not have been able to communicate with. One friend even saw it as a savior for her as she found it difficult to get out. One of my friends, however, felt that he became less sociable in the analogue world and that "the quota of communication was satisfied via Facebook", as he expressed it.

I recently saw a fellow writer complaining on Facebook. Her plan was to take a one-month time-out from the platform. She felt that she needed a break to be able to prioritize other things. But she also expressed doubts about her decision as she felt Facebook to be positive in her life. Why should she abandon something that added value to her life? After encouragement from friends, she decided to end her digital detox. The alternative was for her to start planning her Facebook use instead. My recommendation to her was to take a shorter time-out one day a week.

I believe she captured the crux of the paradox. We want to be sociable with other people online, but we also want an analogue life that is not diminished by social media. One of my friends expressed it powerfully "... to be dependent upon being sociable".

Does the use of social media make you more or less sociable? Do you have any strategies for preventing your analogue and online lives from clashing?

Selfie mania

Prior to the digital camera, we rationed the number of photos we took. We had, perhaps, 36 pictures in a roll which meant that we had to be selective with what we photographed. These days, we can go overboard with "film" since our mobiles have better memory capacity for each day. This means that we can afford to photograph almost everything we see: cups of coffee, food, cats and sunsets. Everything ends up in our picture storage and often in our social media accounts.

An important part of social media culture is to take pictures of yourself and together with others. It is a way of showing others what you are doing. You go to the gym, climb a mountain, or have a drink with someone special. On holiday, it may feel especially important to prove to others that we really are in this exotic place, much like when we used to send postcard to one another.

According to an Indian study, there were as many as 259 selfie-related deaths around the world between 2011 and 2017. A common denominator has been that the victims have seemed to have wanted to optimize their selfies. The goal was to get a picture of themselves in a challenging situation. It is easy to assume that the reason for this lethal behavior is the hunt for likes – you believe that the more challenging the selfie situation, the more people will like the picture. Social media leading to death is, of course, extreme, but when the hunt for the perfect picture goes too far, it can be a warning that you may have developed an addiction.

Alicia Vikander, one of Sweden's most successful actresses, spoke

When the selfie stick was launched, it became an overnight success. It has become a symbol of the phenomena of taking self-portraits. But can this become too extreme? Does it feed a narcissistic personality where the ego takes center stage?

There have been hundreds of deaths around the world where selfies have been a probable cause. People have fallen from cliffs and been run down by trains and cars. There have also been drownings and incidents with dangerous animals.

about selfies in an interview with the talk show host Skavlan. She is frequently recognized, and a fan once wanted a selfie with her. Alicia thought that being in a picture was boring and wanted to talk instead, so she said: "Hi, what's your name? Why don't we talk instead?" Rather than being happy at the possibility of chatting with their idol, the fan became upset.

When I had the chance to meet one of my great idols, Leonard Cohen, I chose not to photograph him. Instead, I spoke to him for a while and got his autograph. It was a far better experience than chasing a picture just so I could show to people, as a trophy.

When researchers have analyzed this phenomenon, they have noticed dependency-like behavior. It is as though some people become obsessed with posting selfies, perhaps more and more each day. I see selfies as an important part of the puzzle in understanding social media addiction. You take a picture and post it in order to get likes. Large numbers of likes make you happy and make you feel validated. You want to experience this again and the vicious circle begins.

How many selfies and photos do you take with your mobile? Have you ever felt a compulsion to do so, or is it purely positive?

Accessibility feeds addiction

Today, over half of the world's population are connected, and almost as many are using social media. Almost 70 percent have access to a mobile, which is the most common way of staying connected. Therefore, the gateway to social media is practically always open, to a large part of the world's population.

When the internet was in its infancy, access to social media was limited. Internet speed was far from today's lightning-quick connection. At the same time, we had relatively few screens, a desktop computer was often shared by a whole family. A digital queue was a common scenario. A parent's internet banking had to compete with the children's gaming. Today, several screens, all with connection to the internet, are common. In many families, access is huge. There may be a desktop, a laptop for work or school, a tablet, a smart TV and a mobile each. These days, there are also smart watches with a screen and internet connection. This means that most people have continuous access to at least one screen, which increases the risk of becoming hooked, since easy accessibility is an important factor in developing an addiction.

When our mobile phones developed into small computers, social media had a huge breakthrough. The parallel development of the iPhone (2007) and Facebook (2004) led to the instant popularity of being social on Facebook, using your phone. A user no longer needed a computer – we literally had social media in our pockets wherever we were. Suddenly we had access to social media around the clock. These days, we see people walking, cycling and driving with a mobile stuck to their hands. The temptation is often social media, why should we wait to check our feed?

Does this create any problems? Yes, we can see people who miss out on a sunset or a physical meeting with another person. A baby crying whilst its parent is checking Instagram. The worst cases are when accidents happen. There have been many traffic accidents where mobile use has been a factor. I was once hit by a bike, for instance. I was waiting at a pedestrian crossing and crossed when the light turned green. I glanced at my mobile and, at the last minute, noticed a cyclist at full speed. He, too, was staring at his screen and had missed that the lights had turned red for him. The cyclist braked and I jumped backwards, but the bike still ran over my foot. It turned out the cyclist was a friend from my gym. We apologized to one another, and stated that there was no major harm done. I escaped with just a sore toe. But what if it had been a truck instead...

On 1st February 2018, a law was passed in Sweden making it illegal to have a mobile in your hand whilst driving. Despite this, I see dangerous situations every day where a driver is more focused on his mobile than the traffic.

What pros and cons do you see in having social media on your phone?
Have you ever tried removing your social media apps?
How did it feel?

4. Social media addiction

What is an addiction?

The word addiction can mean different things. I can joke about being addicted to risotto. By this, I mean that I love this incredible dish, but I would, of course, survive without it if I had to.

Then there are addictions that refer to normal use transferring into a state of illness. In such cases, it is a psychological state where a person continues with a certain behavior or with using certain substances irrespective of any negative consequences. This can be anything from nicotine addiction to video game addiction. In these cases, the person has lost control. The drug or behavior dominates, and the conscious will takes second place.

If the results from research are reliable, an addiction can be classified as a clinical diagnosis. In such cases, there are clear criteria normally listed in DSM (Diagnostic and Statistical Manual), issued by the American Psychiatric Association or in the IDC (International Statistical Classification of Diseases and Health Problems), issued by the WHO. This means that, as an addiction expert, I can conduct a test to determine whether a person has an addiction or not. Usually, detailed questionnaires are used, leading to an objective assessment and thereby the correct treatment.

Not all addictions are classed as clinical diagnoses. In these cases, we can still discuss the phenomena as a dependency. This was the case with video game addiction, which has been classed as a diagnosis by the WHO since May 2019. Long before this, professionals like me, parents, gamers and other people, determined that games could be addictive. Research and science take time. The long-term studies are often the interesting ones. So, it is important to be careful about classifying diagnoses.

Addictions are usually split into two groups: substance addictions and behavioral addictions.

Substance addictions

This refers to older and accepted states of addiction. The addict uses some kind of substance, for example alcohol, tobacco or narcotics. These states of dependency are included in DSM or IDC with clear criteria. It is possible to test and determine if a person has this type of addiction.

With substance addiction, both psychological and physical changes occur. The physical abstinence becomes tangible. An addict can demonstrate shaking and headaches if they cannot take the substance they are dependent upon. If, like me, you are dependent upon caffeine, perhaps you have experienced a light headache if you have missed out on your daily coffee? It may sound harmless, since the headache disappears when you have your coffee, but substance addictions can sometimes become extremely serious. If, for example, you are addicted to heroin, an overdose can lead to sudden death.

Behavioral addictions

For several years now, there has developed a new type of addiction called behavioral addiction. This is all about behavior and not substances. Gambling and video game addictions are two examples. The difference to substance addiction is that the user does not consume anything, instead it is the behavior that becomes the addiction.

The criteria for behavior addictions are similar to those used in substance addictions which means that all addictions have a similar core. But there are also differences: is the phenomenon legal or illegal? Are there any wider uses with positive effects? Does society want the phenomenon to cease or not? Is it a part of our culture? Amongst other reasons, this is why I believe that all addictions should be examined from their own unique perspectives.

During my years as a dependency expert, I have focused more and more on the person behind the addiction, which provides a more dignified approach. Sometimes there is too much emphasis on the addictive behavior. It is better to focus on the person's positive traits, so that he or she can put the addiction to one side. It is possible to escape a dependency, regardless of whether it is alcohol or a digital addiction.

So, what about social media? It is increasingly described as a modern digital addiction, similar to video game addiction. The research is relatively new and limited, which means that social media addiction has not yet been classed as a clinical diagnosis. But we still need to study the negative effects that can occur during excessive use of social media and try to create a reasonable approach to lessen damage and prevent problems. There are some researchers who have studied social media addiction, presenting phenomena which show that even social media can cause an addiction. What happens in our reward system in the brain is very similar to what happens in other addictions. Regardless of whether you take a drink or receive a like.

Signs of social media addiction

Negative consequences

One of the basic criteria for an addiction is the cause of negative consequences. It can mean work, studies, relationships and spare time being affected in a way that becomes a problem for you or other people. It is not an addiction just because it takes up a lot of your time.

These days we normally have social media on our mobiles and, since access to our mobile is constant, we can be constantly burning time. At the gym, when posting a picture of you exercising, at work when your meeting is interrupted by someone sending you a snap, or when cooking; as when I burnt my risotto. Risotto requires constant stirring, but I could suddenly smell something burning. What had happened? I had received a notification on my mobile that someone had commented on something I had posted in an authors' group. I just "had to check" but, of course, became caught up in the discussion. And the risotto? Of course, I forgot all about it and had to start over. A burnt risotto cannot be saved.

When social media clashes with other things, such as my burnt risotto, it is a negative consequence. The same goes for the screaming child whose parent is buried in their mobile. The child has to scream even louder in order to be heard. According to psychologist Jakob Jonsson, there is a risk of problems with bonding if the child needs to scream louder and louder in order to get attention. It can damage its trust in adults, which can result in long-term negative consequences for the child.

When talking to students about social media, everyone agrees that it often takes too much time away from other things, more than they would like. "I would rather paint and read books", said one student. She had occasionally removed Instagram in order to focus on her interests "but I always return".

It is exactly this type of thing that can be the downside of social media. Not the fact that it is time consuming, but that it lures us away from other things that we would rather have done. That it over-rules other activities.

But doesn't the student have a choice? Her own theory of why she let it take control of her time was: "social media is designed to trap you; it is very difficult to resist the pressure". She described the thing that I had also experienced: a dependency that takes prece-dence over your own free will. Social media rules over you, when it should be you who is in charge. Here, loss of control comes in. For when you lose control, it is much easier to leave your activities and slide over to social media.

What the student told me was nothing that was unique to her. The fact is, I believe it is one of the biggest downsides to social media, we feel manipulated to do things that we hadn't really planned to do.

Focus and preoccupation
All addicts are conscious of one thing above all. It is to think, plan and arrange their addiction. This is true of the alcoholic who makes sure that someone else can drive home from the party, or the gamer who turns down the family holiday, from fear of ending up in a digi-tal wasteland, and would rather stay at home with a stable broad-band connection.

This warning sign is probably the first thing that those around you will notice. You think, plan and adapt your life with social media in mind, even when you are not online. A beautifully presented meal is primarily a potential Instagram picture – not an enjoyable meal.

As soon as the opportunity arises, the fingers slide over the mobile screen, as if pulled there by some magical force. The feeling of "it just happens" is common.

I call it the mobile bubble, when what happens in the mobile apps becomes the most important thing in life. I have been there myself. At worst, I spent every possible moment of free time checking Facebook and Jodel. A couple of minutes whilst waiting for a bus, or on the toilet. "Don't get stuck in your mobile", my partner used to say when my visits to the bathroom became longer and longer. Whenever I saw something interesting, I immediately thought: "this would look good on Facebook".

Abstinence

Abstinence is the phenomenon that occurs when a person tries to rid themselves of their addiction. Abstinence occurs when a substance is not taken, such as with alcohol addiction; or a behavior ceases, such as when someone stops gambling or using social media. This can cause both physical and psychological problems.

Becoming abstinent is a serious warning sign. A person without addiction has no problem taking a break from social media. It shows a healthy use where the person is in control. But for someone with a problem, abstinence can feel both strange and unpleasant, a state most of us would wish to avoid. Irritation, stress and melancholy are obvious signs.

When my previous mobile broke, it took some time until my new one was set up. I experienced clear signs of stress by not being able to check Facebook. I became nervous and easily irritated. It was the same feeling as when the TV plays up during live broadcasts; I might miss something important. In order to avoid my abstinence, I wanted to return to using Facebook as soon as possible. Had it been a few years earlier, I would have welcomed a well-needed break. But during the time of my addiction, it was simply stressful.

There are two types of abstinence. The one that occurs involuntarily, such as in my case with my broken phone. The other type is that if I choose to do a digital detox. In this case it is easier to deal with the abstinence as I have chosen to detox myself.

Abstinence from behavioral addictions are different to substance addictions, since no chemical substance needs to leave the body. It is all about a habit and a passing psychological state. Despite this difference, a psychological abstinence is perceived as oppressive. But abstinence is something that stops after a while; it is not a permanent damage. In my case, it took about a week to rid myself of the abstinence from social media.

Raising your tolerance

Wanting more of something is a classic sign of an addiction. Raising your tolerance means that the addict must gradually increase his or her intake in order to reach the same level as before. It can mean better games, more powerful drugs, larger amounts of alcohol or more social media.

One example that many people can relate to is alcohol. The first time a person drinks, only a small amount is needed to have an effect. A strong beer can create a feeling of euphoria in a beginner. The more a person drinks, the more is needed to relive the first intoxication. Therefore, we can see heavy drinkers who are hardly affected at all, even from high amounts of alcohol. The body has simply gotten used to the alcohol and can withstand more.

I see similar raises in tolerance in digital addiction, people going from low-level use to manic zombie scrolling.

My first faltering steps into social media comprised the casual checking of Facebook, Instagram and Twitter. To begin with it was just a couple of times a week. As time went on, I made more friends on Facebook, tried new platforms and joined lots of groups. I wanted more. At its worst, I spent several hours a day discussing, reading posts and posting pictures. I needed more and more experiences to feel satisfied. The treacherous thing about this warning sign is that the change comes creeping up. It does not happen overnight, but gradually over a longer period.

Denial

There is a humorous expression with a serious undertone about gambling addiction: "I am not addicted, I can stop gambling whenever I want, wanna bet?"

I often hear similar expressions from clients with digital addiction. They believe they have complete control over their lives online, when in reality they show several warning signs of being addicted. In their world they are in control, instead believing it is the people around them who do not understand. The person denies any problem whatsoever.

Denial comes from a lack of insight; the addict does not understand that he or she is caught in a vicious circle. This is an important component in a dependency. If people close to you have opinions, denial becomes a protective measure, an armor to enable you to maintain your behavior. There is no bad intention, it is merely a natural defense.

This happened to me at the height of my social media use. During this period, I claimed to be doing research for my next book. It was, indeed, true, but I realized afterwards that I used it as a legitimate reason for using my mobile.

Lies

In my professional role, I have seen many examples of addicts lying in order to protect their addiction. A client of mine had used his parents' cash card, without their permission, to buy things for his games. It was a lot of money and the boy was the only one in the family who played. It was obvious who was guilty. Despite this, he tried to lie his way out with unbelievable stories.

If a previously honest and decent person turns to lies, it can be painful for those around him. It can feel as though a new personality has taken over. The lies can trigger conflicts in the family, workgroup or amongst friends. When it comes to social media use on a mobile, it is easy to do it in secret, because it is easy to claim something that is difficult for others to check.

Unfortunately, even I have displayed this unpleasant behavior. "No, I am not checking Facebook, I am reading an important work email." This is what I told my family during a meal in order to defend my mobile use – a clear example of wanting to protect my addiction.

When an addict starts to lie, it is often unconsciously. It is not about hurting those around him, but the lie is a way of being able to continue the addiction. To me, my lie became a turning point, that was when I realized that I was hooked.

Losing control

The first phase, long before an addiction develops, is called use. You are in control of your drinking, gambling or scrolling on social media. You sometimes read, post, like and share. None of these things clash with anything else in your life. At this stage, most people feel that social media can be a small and natural part of life.

But what happens when it starts to go out of control? Then, despite being busy with other things, you may find yourself zombie-scrolling. Maybe you just had to check a like or comment, but after ten minutes you realize that you have ended up checking other things as well.

The possibility of receiving a notification creates a bigger risk of losing control. If the mobile notifies you of a message, you are at risk of stopping what you are doing. The mobile chooses when you pick it up, not the other way around. If you always end up allowing impulses to dominate, you could end up in a position feeling powerless. You are no longer in control.

The feeling when you lose control is often one of resignation at not being able to resist temptation. After a while you lose track of time. You become immersed in the activity and time simply slips away.

My own attempts at balancing my use of social media often failed, which shows that I had lost control. Facebook dominated me, not the other way around. The feeling of being stuck online from morning to evening felt more and more unpleasant. I realized my family had been right, I was addicted.

Relapse

Relapse is when a person returns to an old pattern of behavior. Of all the cases of addiction I have worked with, there are very few who have never relapsed. Sometimes it is just a temporary return to the old behavior, it can be as a test to see how it was to smoke, drink or gamble. Many people talk about a "pull" back, that they want to try one last time before they definitely change their behavior. In other cases, it may mean ending up on a slippery slope, that the person resumes his old addictive behavior without the will to change.

For relatives, relapse can feel hopeless. It is like the tape being rewound back to when the situation was at its worst. This way of thinking can create negative expectations. I often meet relatives who, during a relapse, immediately lose hope, creating a negative feeling that is then passed on to the person with the addiction. There is then a risk that the person loses their incentive and instead returns to and increases their addiction. But I have full respect for the fact that relatives can often become co-dependent and thereby fall easily into a negative spiral.

If you relapse, I do not think you should feel that you have failed. That is rarely the way forward. It's better to start anew. A relapse proves how deeply addicted you are, which can make you take your addiction more seriously. We can also learn a lot from a relapse. In what situations do they occur? What did I do that led to the relapse? How can I prevent new ones from occurring? It is important to recognize when I "take" a relapse. I do not "get" it from some invisible force. If you realize it, you also understand that you have the power to make your own choices.

I have often said to myself: This weekend I shall not check Facebook at all. After only a few hours, I have broken my own promise. When I recently changed my mobile phone, I did a test. I did not install the Facebook app on the new phone. The plan was to check Facebook only on my desktop computer. How long do you think it lasted? One day. Because I was doing research for my book and I could miss important information. I had the opportunity to re-evaluate my plan and came to the conclusion that I had set the bar too high. This was not the way to get rid of my addiction.

Conflicts with loved ones

All types of addictions and dependencies affect the environment. Family, friends, colleagues and schoolmates. The difference in how hard others are affected depends on what type of addiction is involved. In the case of serious drug abuse, relationships can become extremely strained. But even spending too much time on the internet can lead to conflict.

Imagine a person who always checks his mobile whilst having dinner at home with his family. Everyone points it out, yet the person continues. In the end, it can escalate to a larger conflict. Instead of embracing the criticism, the person argues against it. The fact that it is mentioned by your closest relatives and friends is often a typical warning sign. Because if you are in the center of your mobile bubble, you will be oblivious to your own dependency. But your loved ones are not and can see if you are beginning to slide into addiction.

"Can't you stop checking Facebook now dad?" was something I often heard from my children during the period when I was hooked. My answer was always some kind of defense that often ended in an argument. In hindsight, I can see that this was ridiculous. Was it worth it? Hardly. It should be clarified here that the degree by which relationships are affected depends upon how strong they are deep down. I sometimes meet families where the relationships are already strained. Then, disagreements about social media can be the straw that breaks the camel's back. But, if the relationships are strong, it may be easier to resolve possible new problems associated with the addiction.

Digital stress and mental ill-health
Mental ill-health is on the rise around the world. Over the last few years, the increase has been about 50 percent. More and more people seek help for depression, anxiety, social phobia and other conditions. The queues to psychiatric units are long. Many people seem to be stressed by today's lifestyle.

Previously, when reading a magazine or watching the news, there was always an end state. However, our digital input is never-ending. We have constant access to news, emails and social media. I have, myself, experienced digital stress. Liking friends' posts and reading comments have felt like a compulsion, like if not doing it was not okay. Things that I have previously always enjoyed, like congratulating somebody on their birthday, suddenly felt like a duty. I noticed that I was constantly exposing my brain to digital stimuli. Every free moment, my brain was awash with information.

Even the flow of news felt important to keep abreast of. New terror attacks, the risk of war, interest rates. I wanted to know everything now and not later. There is a logical explanation to this behavior. It is supposedly a remaining survival strategy from the time when we lived in caves. Back then, we had to keep an eye on the fire, predators and other things that could threaten our existence. In a similar way, we can see that the modern human, through his mobile, has a strong radar towards his surroundings. We can scan everything: the local weather through a weather app, and how my relative on the other side of the world is doing via Instagram.

But the digital stress led to me not getting the necessary micropauses in my daily life. Entry codes and PIN codes could stress me out. It was as though my brain had become overloaded by all things digital. I sometimes had an impulse to throw my mobile in the lake. Of course, I didn't, but the longing for a lost analogue time was ever-present.

Typical of most dependencies is the experiencing of a feeling of emptiness. It can occur when a person leaves his drug or his behavior and starts to show signs of depression. This can be a sign that the activity has previously filled an important function.

I see this in all types of clients. For example, I have met gamers who have difficulty finding other fun alternatives to gaming. When they stop playing, they become low and feel as though life is boring. We see the same effect in those who are very active on social media, which fills an important need for their social relationships. When this channel is removed, it is natural to feel bad, especially if you do not have the possibility of replacing the contacts in the analogue world.

Escapist behavior could also be a part of the equation. If a person who is not feeling well misuses something to temporarily numb his feelings, the addiction becomes an escape and, if the addiction is treated, the basic problem still remains.

When speaking to researcher Fred Nyberg, he emphasized the risks of becoming caught behind a screen. For young people this can result in diminished social skills. They do not develop the ability to read body language and sometimes have less body contact. This can lead to the level of oxytocin to decrease. This is one of the body's own happy hormones released during direct body contact; such as a handshake or a hug.

FOMO – Fear of Missing Out

A phenomenon regarding social media addiction is a fear of missing something. It can lead to you feeling forced to be constantly online, that you must be 100 percent up-to-date on your platforms. This then leads to the next dilemma; how do you deal with all the invitations to events, lectures and parties? Perhaps you start to say yes to everything. If you say no, you may miss something amazing. Or will you?

Usually, you can "survive" without knowing everything that goes on, but the feeling of FOMO can make you believe that you really are missing out on important things. This, of course, is an impossible equation. You cannot physically be everywhere. Furthermore, it is not just the information in our mobiles that feeds FOMO. I believe it is our entire modern way of life that has created this vicious circle. Everything must happen at lightning speed and we feel pressurized to be everywhere.

A student once told me that, because all of her friends used social media, she felt left out if she didn't. A typical example of peer pressure and sign of FOMO.

A friend of hers said the opposite: "If I sit home alone, I can see where my friends are and go there and socialize." This was one of her reasons to remain on the platforms. She didn't want to be alone. It is a good example displaying the two sides of social media. It can cause both anxiety and reduce loneliness.

When I go to the countryside to be alone and write, I use social media in a similar way. Of course, it is nice to be able to focus on writing my book, but it can also be boring to be alone. Then I can easily communicate via Facebook and therefore experience social belonging. Just like when I go to the gym and chat to the people I meet.

I too have been affected by FOMO. I felt pressurized to keep a check on my social media feed. I was afraid of missing something on Facebook, which meant I had to keep a close eye on my mobile. It fed my addiction and was one of the reasons that I became hooked.

Sleeping problems

Good sleep is vital for human beings. The brain needs to revitalize, and long-term sleeping problems can lead to both physical and psychological problems. It can lead to difficulties in concentrating, irritability and stomach problems.

When I examine new clients, I look into their sleep habits amongst other things. My view is that many people sleep too little, irregularly and have difficulty going to sleep. They rarely wake up rested. When we find out about their screen habits, we see that most of them take their mobiles to bed. They play games, check YouTube and visit social media. It is common to not fall asleep until the middle of the night, since they cannot tear themselves away from their screens.

Having your mobile in bed is common amongst both young people and adults. I often talk to people who see it as natural to be able to communicate in the middle of the night. A young man I spoke to said that it was down to a sense of responsibility to his friends; if something happened and they needed help. When I asked him if the friends really were people in need, and he admitted that it was not the case. Rather, it was a feeling of never wanting to really close down. Just like an emergency phone number – always on standby.

How do the actual screens affect our sleep? The blue light from screens, combined with your brain being in overdrive rather than relaxing, can lead to you sleeping less and having an unsettled sleep. It can cause you to never feel properly rested.

Physical problems

Apart from the mental problems caused by the excessive use of social media, it can also cause physical problems. When I spoke to a physiotherapist, he told me about new ailments that had emerged at his surgery: SMS thumbs and iHunch. Young people come to him with physical ailments previously only found in elderly factory workers. The cause is the repetitive movement of their fingers on the screen and that most people lower their heads in an unnatural and position when they have their screens at stomach height. It is better to raise your screen to eye-level and exercise your fingers between writing an SMS.

Another negative effect is the rise in sitting still in a sedentary position. Of course, we can use the mobile when we exercise with the help of an app, or play games such as Pokémon GO, with the aim of going out for a walk. But, in reality, it is clear that many people end up on the sofa with their screen. Social media keeps us there. Hour after hour. This can create long-term and serious problems, since sitting still is a risk factor for heart and vascular disorders, diabetes and obesity.

Eye doctors and opticians can see an increase in children with different types of eye problems. They believe that too much screen time can be the cause and we can only speculate about how this will affect the children in later life.

Do you recognize any of these warning signs with regards to your own life on social media?

User zones for social media

As a pioneer in video game addiction, I introduced the zone model above. There were several reasons. Partly, it was to highlight that we had not yet had a clinical diagnosis for video game addiction, and partly from an educational point of view – I wanted to make it clearer and easier to understand how an addiction can develop.

My model is based on the idea that we can travel between zones, that people are able to break their negative behaviors. If the addiction went as far as the yellow or red zone, you can reverse to the green or white zone. Instead of focusing on the negative side of your addiction, you can take a positive view, you can make a change. I often receive emails from gamers or their relatives who have used the zone model to judge make an assumption of where they are.

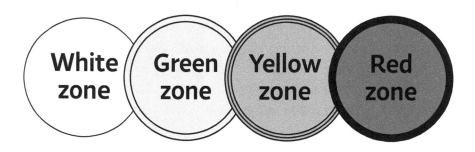

White zone – non user

If you are in the white zone, it means that you do not use social media at all. Being outside of social media is fairly uncommon and a frequently asked question is whether you can be in the white zone and still have a rich and functioning social life?

The simple answer is: Of course we can. Having an Instagram or Facebook account is not an obligation. I have several friends and relatives who are in this zone and who are satisfied with that. They are digital outcasts and/or emigrants who have chosen to either not join or to no longer remain.

If you are in the white zone, you are not at any risk of developing a problem. If you are not using anything, you cannot experience its negative effects. The possible price to pay is that you may miss the potential benefits of controlled use. Just as if you choose not to drink coffee or not to gamble.

Green zone – digital balance

Being in the green zone, social media brings mainly positive effects. You feel that social media brings you a richer social life, entertains you, provides you with information, improves your business, or helps you if you feel unwell. A characteristic of being in the green zone is that you can control your use. You are in control and you can take breaks or stop without any problems.

When discussing social media, we need to remember that many people can handle it without it creating negative consequences. Their use is mainly positive. If your social media use is "green", there is no need to change your habits.

Yellow zone – at-risk user

In the yellow zone, negative consequences begin to appear. Those close to you may begin to complain about your mobile behavior at the dinner table. When you should be working or studying, you frequently end up using your platforms. You feel pressurized to check your feed and post more and more. This is where quick clicks and kicks provide you with increasing dopamine effects. The time you spend on social media is increasing.

You have a sneaking suspicion that you are no longer in control. You begin to misuse and experience negative effects. At this point, the user is still able to partly control their behavior. If you are in this zone, you can usually return to the green zone, just like someone who has started to drink a little too much alcohol and begins to see the warning signs of abuse.

Red zone – addiction

Now we have arrived at the end station. In the red zone you are extremely focused on social media, which takes up almost every waking moment. Your work, school, family and spare time are suffering, and you experience several of the negative consequences associated with your use.

A common feeling in the red zone is one of unease and a feeling that it is less fun. It feels as though you are being forced to be active and it is clear that you have lost control. It is the pursuit of new kicks that control you, rather than you making conscious choices. But, despite the negative consequences, the behavior continues. At this point it is harder to break free and outside help may be needed. But rewinding the tape and regaining control is possible, although it does take motivation and time.

Model of social media addiction

In order to understand how an addiction develops, I have created a model for social media addiction. It shows which factors create and maintain an addiction.

First and foremost, there are different background factors that can affect the risk of becoming hooked on social media. It might be that you belong to a risk group or you are at heightened risk from peer pressure.

Then there are the types of platforms, number of screens and which accounts you follow. How much you use these services is important. And here you can also make choices.

The dopamine effect comes automatically whether you want it or not. Dopamine is a major reason for why we become hooked in an addiction. It is a chemical reaction in the brain that is difficult for us to influence. Therefore, we should not feel guilt or shame if we become addicted.

At the end of the model are the negative consequences. What is interesting is that the behavior continues despite knowledge of the negative effects. In that phase, will is subordinate to the addiction. Social media rules you and your behavior.

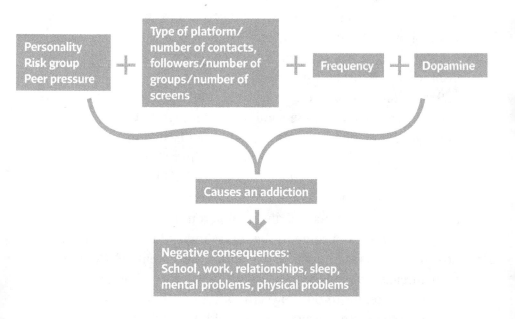

As you can see, several different factors determine how an addiction develops. For this very reason, it is important to have a holistic view of these complex phenomena.

Screen conflicts

Although we still argue about who takes out the rubbish or who washes the dishes, over the last few years a new battlefield has emerged. It is centered around the use of screens.

In many families, there are screen conflicts. Everyone seems to have opinions on one another's online lives. Whether or not dad should check Facebook at the dinner table, if mum's Instagram takes up too much time, if the children should disconnect from Snapchat so they can get enough sleep, if it is a good idea to watch YouTube whilst doing homework, and so on. Everywhere there seems to be discussions and conflicts. It is important to realize that this is relevant for all ages. The younger generation often receives unfair criticism when it is just as much an adult problem.

Some conflicts can be simple bickering amongst adults. About whether or not the mobile should be there when watching TV or at the breakfast table. It often turns into a discussion about whose rules apply. Is it okay to double-screen at the TV? Is reading a newspaper better than reading the news on your mobile?

As an advisor, I also see more serious conflicts that can degenerate. Imagine a family having dinner. A parent tells their child to put away the screen and come to the table. The child nods but continues to send snaps and watch YouTube. The parent tells the child more forcibly. The child responds with: "soon, I'm just gonna...", but makes no attempt to put down the screen. The parent gets angry and takes the screen away from the child. The child, who was in the middle of a conversation with a friend, becomes furious, runs up to the parent and tries to snatch the screen from his parent's hands. A moment later, the screen falls on the floor and breaks. A sad and angry child is crying in its bed whilst the parent sits and eats alone. A battle without a winner.

Unfortunately, this scenario is commonplace amongst the families I meet. I have also been told by my children and partner that I should put my phone away, and this used to lead to unnecessary conflict.

Are these conflicts any different to the arguments of the past where screens were not involved? Yes, in a way. For these types of behavior apply to us all, since most of us have an online presence. The platforms might differ, but the phenomena of wanting to be online is the same whether it is Snapchat, Instagram or Facebook.

I believe the reason for many of our arguments is that we have not yet found the cultural frameworks for handling it. We must remember that the internet, social media and mobiles have only recently come into our lives. Unlike alcohol, table manners and birthday celebrations, we simply have not had the time to discuss what values and limits should apply.

The more we talk to each other, the easier it is to prevent these problems. One of my popular suggestions for families is to agree on a digital policy. That is to say, talk through what should apply at the dinner table, whilst watching TV and in other situations where conflicts often arise in that particular family. If we do, many of these fractions can be avoided.

Parents are often concerned at their children spending so much time alone. "They just sit there in front of their screens," I often hear. But are they really alone? Often, they are enjoying a rich social life through games and social media – as I previously mentioned, the internet has become the young person's youth club. The internet is where they hang out and meet with friends. For this reason, the children do not feel particularly isolated. They have a rich life, but it is online. This misunderstanding often leads to unnecessary conflicts between children and adults.

The solution is for parents to find out what their children are doing. Most children like their parents to be interested, that they care about their interests and activities. This is usually a given with sporty children – when parents drive them to training, go to matches and cheer them on. But what about the children's digital habits? Do adults take the same interest in their children's lives online? Do parents keep as much track there? Not necessarily. I often meet parents who know nothing about their children's lives online, which platforms they are spending time on and which games they play. But they should. For the children, social media provides a natural meeting place and they are exposed to certain risks. The more you talk about the internet with your child, the greater the possibility of understanding one another and thereby avoiding unnecessary conflicts.

Digital freedom or parental control?

What should parents do? Leave the kids alone, or have complete control of how they use social media? The very least you can do as a parent is to find out which platforms your child is active on and try them for yourself. An obvious question at the dinner table should be: "How was your day online?" in order to open a dialogue about things that can happen online – both positive phenomena such as friendship, but also how we should behave towards one another, what personal information is okay to give out and to whom. Talking about the internet should be as natural as talking about their day at school.

One sensitive issue is whether we should be friends with our children on Facebook and follow each other on Instagram? If we have adult children, this is rarely a problem, as the parent's presence is often accepted. But do teenagers want their parents to know everything about their online lives? Well, here we should consider digital freedom. I remember when I was a child, building dens in the woods. I was with my friends, without adult supervision. The point was that no adults knew what we were doing. It is a natural process for children to free themselves from the beady eyes of adults' and their control, and what parent would choose to sit in the corner of a youth club watching everything their child said or did? If they did, it would certainly not be appreciated by the child. I believe the youth of today have the same desire for freedom that I had myself. They want to be able to surf without being constantly watched over and controlled, they want to be trusted.

Therefore, a parent should safeguard their children's digital freedom. There is, of course, a difference between whether it is young children or teenagers. The younger the child is, the more insight the parent should have. But as the child grows older, we must dare to let go as we do with most other things regarding our children. I believe that one of the keys to successful digital parenting, is to take different approaches depending on the child's age.

Online role models

Most people who have contact with children, have probably realized that they do not always do as adults say. But children often mimic behaviors. If you have children around you, as do parents, teachers or relatives, you can fill an important function by being an online role model. As an adult, you can begin by studying your own online behavior. Set a good example by sometimes putting away your mobile and reflecting on when and how you use it. I often see adults scolding their children because they play too much games. At the same time, they themselves have the mobile phone glued to their hand. You can easily set a good example creating your own digital balance. Live as you learn.

Some families decide on days when they are completely offline. They try to revert back to the old ways of socializing. Board games are dusted off, the football comes out and a great movie at the cinema is enjoyed without mobiles. Personally, I have always thought that the best thing is to find alternatives where the digital gets a natural rest. Going to the swimming pool or climbing a mountain is best without a mobile in your hand. Moreover, you do something fun which means that you do not miss social media.

Keep in mind that things can be experienced in a family without having to upload everything online. Often the experience can be both more intense and feel more exclusive if not every detail is documented. It creates a stronger bond if the rest of the world cannot see what you have been doing.

Are there any screen conflicts in your family, at work or amongst your friends?
Do you have any ways of dealing with it?

5. Risk groups

Having worked with digital addiction over the years, I have been able to distinguish some groups that are particularly at risk of becoming addicted. When I talk to colleagues, they have similar experiences. It seems that it is easier for certain people to get hooked on social media than others.

Identifying risk groups has several advantages. If you are in a risk group, you can try to be more vigilant in order to not become dependent. If you are a relative, you may be able to detect warning signs earlier and help if it starts to grow out of control. There is also the opportunity to work preventively through different organizations, schools and authorities, like the Swedish national association Attention, which deals with children who have different neuropsychiatric disabilities. Young people with neuropsychiatric diagnoses is, according to Attention, online more frequently and for longer periods of time compared to other children. These young people experience clear advantages with using the internet. For example, they can make friends more easily, which they can sometimes find difficult to do in the analogue world.

For these young people, there is often a clear parental concern for the children's difficulties in interpreting information. Therefore, parents often ask for guidance for their children's day-to-day internet use. In my work with digital addictions, there are two key diagnoses that stand out: ADHD and ASD/Asperger.

ADHD

If you have ADHD (Attention Deficit Hyperactiviti Disorder), you may have problems with self-discipline, impulse control, and overactivity. Everything happens at full speed without consideration of the potential consequences. A good friend of mine who has ADHD makes the comparison to a sports car without brakes. You drive at high speed even though you know you will probably drive into a ditch. When it comes to social media, it can mean that you post things without thinking about the consequences. Then, in the worst case, you can wake up with a digital hangover, when you find that you have posted things that you regret afterwards.

Another aspect of ADHD is the phenomenon of hyper focus. This means that the person is so focused on an activity that they are unaware of what is happening around them. I have had clients where games and social media have caused them to miss a knock at the door or to forget to go the bathroom. It can be a positive force to be strongly focused, particularly in exercising, entrepreneurship and such like, but if everything revolves around social media, it is easy for school, work and other important things to suffer.

I often meet clients with ADHD who triple-screen. They have three different screens running at the same time as they mix gaming, social media and watching a movie. Of course, this behavior creates a risk that their experience becomes fragmented and that it feeds a negative behavior. Those with ADHD should be extra vigilant with their digital life so that it does not get out of control.

ASD/Asperger

Asperger's syndrome is another type of neuropsychiatric condition. Today, it is commonly referred to as ASD (Autism Spectrum Disorder) but the term Asperger is likely to remain.

People with this diagnosis may have problems interpreting facial expressions and body language. Metaphors, ambiguities and messages "between the lines" can also be difficult to understand. Words are often interpreted literally, which means that there can be misunderstandings in social situations and communication.

Another phenomenon is that a person with ASD often has special interests that they can become excessively focused on. If you have digital interests, it can be difficult to limit them. I have had clients with ASD who see their digital activity as the primary thing in life. It almost becomes like a job that they focus on. If you have ASD, there is an increased risk of getting hooked online. People with ASD often prefer to socialize digitally. They then avoid hugs, eye contact, the smell of sweat and other things that they might otherwise perceive as unpleasant. Digital communication can have a clearer focus, especially given that body language and voice tones disappear completely.

I have had online contact with people with ASD who communicate easily, but where the same person can appear insecure and quiet when face-to-face. Increased self-confidence online gives a sense of relief at finally enjoying good social relationships. In such cases, the use of digital communication can be an obvious choice, regardless of whether it is via a game or social media. There are also Facebook groups where the participants share a diagnosis, which is a way of finding like-minded people who "speak the same language".

A person with ASD can benefit greatly from social media, but they also need to be vigilant. Otherwise, the risk is that online contact becomes the only social contact they have.

Kick seekers

Some people seem to have a tendency to develop different dependencies primarily because they are constantly looking for a new kick. During my many years as an addiction expert, I have often met these kick seekers. They seem to be constantly engaged in some kind of addiction or exaggerated behavior. I have met people who switched between alcohol, gambling, criminality and digital addiction. If they stop one addiction, it is usually replaced by another. It is as though the person must always be manically obsessed with something.

When I interviewed dependency researcher Fred Nyberg, he brought up an interesting thesis on kick-seekers. He spoke about an enzyme called monoamine oxidase-B (MAO-B).

There are signs that people with a low level of MAO-B, look for more excitement and adventure, so called "sensations seekers" and if you have a higher level, you can be satisfied with a quieter life. The level of MAO-B remains constant throughout life, or even increase with aging, so we can see even in small children the difference between those who are happy playing quietly in the sandpit and those who start climbing trees. Nyberg suggests that it makes no difference whether the person gets excitement through a police hunt, martial arts or climbing. Or through a digital addiction. The best thing is if you can find an activity which goes no further than being a positive passion, such as exercising or adventurous activities with positive effects and controlled risks. But the line between an addiction and a passion can be very thin.

People with evasive behavior

An addiction can sometimes be a symptom of other, underlying, problems. Social media becomes an escape to avoid problems in their lives outside the digital world. It can be a child who is bullied at school or who has parents who are ill. It can also be adults who are unemployed, suffer from mental illness or who are otherwise socially excluded. Then, the internet and social media can become an escape, a way to forget their difficult everyday lives.

This evasive behavior works in the short-term, but it does not solve the basic problem. Rather, it can aggravate the situation because the person is ignoring the problem. I, myself, have had contact with children who, due to autism, do not function in an ordinary school. If the school is not adapted, the child stays at home and gets hooked on games and in social media. In the short term, it cures the anxiety, but it does not solve the basic problem.

But isn't the occasional escape from reality something that everyone needs? Isn't it a way to recharge your batteries in order to be able to do all the other things that you must do? I can sometimes use social media and games in that way. A short escape from reality as a break from the rest of life. The difference is that I then go back and deal with the washing up or the editing of a manuscript. In these cases, a temporary escape from reality can be positive.

My example of an autistic student is different. Here, escape becomes destructive in the long-term and the excessive abuse of the screen becomes a persistent factor. In this case, the parents' limitation of the child's screen time can be counterproductive. The internet may be the child's only lifeline and cutting it can cause devastating consequences. Adaptation of the school environment may be the only sensible solution.

Children and young people

When the media addresses the problems surrounding social media, it is often children and young people who are at the center, and maybe there is a reason for it. Digital natives are quick to absorb the new technology. Another reason is that children and young people are more exposed and vulnerable to outside influences. They have not really developed their ability to set limits.

In most countries, there is legislation against advertising aimed directly at children. For games, tobacco and other products aimed at adults, there is a clear age limit and even for social media there is often a limit of about 13–16 years. Through new EU legislation, this may become tightened through ID verification and the requirement for parental approval.

The reason why there are limits is that not everything on social media is suitable for children. But today, since the checking of ID has not yet been introduced, we do not know how many minors actually use social media. Social media has become the young people's way of socializing. It is like a giant youth club that is open 24 hours a day. Snaps are sent between classmates, gamers watch when others play games on YouTube and influencers have millions of young followers on Instagram. Peer pressure is enormous. Everyone wants to be where their friends are, and no one wants to be left out. The Internet has become the natural meeting place for young people. This is where you hang out, talk to friends, make new friends, gossip and argue.

But communication and entertainment are good things, aren't they? Yes, but there are pitfalls. Fred Nyberg mentioned an important difference between young and old people, namely that the human brain is not fully developed until the age of 25. Especially the parts that have to do with long-term thinking, risk assessment and understanding of consequences. The reward system is also particularly vulnerable at a young age. It is easier to become addicted if you are young.

Lost focus

Before the digital revolution, students were able to focus in a different way. Pupils sat with a book, paper and pen. Although their studies could be distracted by music from a radio or by a comic book, I often observed that young people maintained a strong focus on their schoolwork. Today, the scenario may be the opposite. Many students I have talked to study like this: On their laptop they are working on an essay. They have their favorite music in their headphones. They have their mobiles next to them the whole time, checking Instagram and Snapchat at every ping. So, what happens to the essay? Obviously, the attention is split between writing, listening to music and checking social media. "It can disrupt my flow", a student said about this. "I often get disrupted. It becomes an interruption and I have to start from scratch. Sometimes I switch off my notifications."

Being disturbed in a study process means that everything takes longer. For each time you are interrupted, you must recap before continuing. "You need to find strategies to be able to handle this," she said. She had successfully tried to put the mobile in another room. Then she worked solidly on her essay for 30 minutes. Then she took a break and went and checked the mobile. A technique that I use myself when I'm writing.

I compare this to when I was at my most active on social media. Then, my flow whilst writing was often interrupted. The reason was not a fire alarm or that the Third World War had broken out. No, the reason was usually that something happened on Facebook and that I felt compelled to check. Immediately. Not when I'd finished writing.

When I spoke to Christina Bengtsson, an expert on focus, she emphasized that focus is sometimes necessary. To achieve certain goals, it is not possible to divide your focus. She, herself, is world champion in shooting, which she could hardly have achieved with a mobile in one hand and a rifle in the other. I, myself, notice a clear difference if I write without any disturbances and then take a leg stretcher to check the mobile. My flow remains intact and the writing is better.

All of this provides an argument for why younger people need guidance in the digital jungle. Smaller children want to live in the here and now and are not always interested in thinking about their future. Play is an important part of growing up, but even games need to have rules. I usually compare online games for kids with sweets; we do not let children into a candy shop and let them eat as much as they want. They would eat themselves to death, because they do not understand that there are consequences. But I often see how adults sprinkle their children with digital technology, and the younger ones can rarely set their own boundaries. In their world, there is no reason to ration their use. Children want to play and be social, which is, of course, positive. Living in the present is important for a child. Adult life with all the responsibilities it entails will come soon enough.

When Snapchat had just been launched, I held a lecture on games and mobiles. The arena was crammed with younger teenagers. I rarely have problems getting attention when I am going to lecture, but here something happened in the audience that I had not seen before. The arena was full of children taking pictures of each other and then laughing like crazy. What was going on? I asked one student what was so funny. "Snapchat" was the answer. As usual, I wanted to know what the kids were doing and, right there and then, I got a quick guide to this unfamiliar new app.

Some countries want a total ban on using mobiles in schools. As an example, in 2018, France introduced a mobile ban in primary and secondary schools. The aim was to improve the students' focus on school work and to reduce internet bullying. It will be exciting to see the results of this in a few years. Sweden also plans to introduce the same ban at school.

In the schools I have visited, I have seen different solutions to the problem of mobile use during class. One solution is to have so-called mobile daycare. The students put their mobiles in a box, where they

Elaine Eksvärd chose kids before klicks

I met with Elaine Eksvärd to hear her views on social media, parenting and entrepreneurship. Elaine is one of Sweden's foremost experts on public speaking and rhetoric. She has written several books on the subject and is a highly sought-after lecturer.

Elaine has been open on social media with regards to her mobile addiction. I contacted her and offered my help. We have had some conversations about her digital life and what she wanted to change. For example, Elaine has been running a parental blog for many years and has been a strong role model for moms. But, on several occasions, she has mentioned that she would rather stop blogging. She has tried but has been persuaded to carry on.

When Elaine is at home with her children, she tries to avoid using social media. She wants to hang out with her children and not see life through a screen. Despite this, it is "easy to get into zombie scrolling". Actually, Elaine wants to quit social media because she doesn't want to feed other people's addictions when she knows she has so many followers. "I think we would be happier if we went back to being analogue again," she says.

My impression of Elaine is that she is fed up with her digital life. At the same time, as most people, she displays a happy life on Instagram. But she can also raise more mundane everyday events. This is a positive aspect of what Elaine blogs about. For life as a parent and entrepreneur can be challenging, and by raising these issues online, people can recognize themselves without the feeling of guilt or shame.

Elaine is also strongly committed to the fight against child sexual abuse. She herself has been a victim, which she has openly described in her book Medan han lever (While he's alive, translator's note). Elaine often uses social media as a tool to make her voice heard and to form opinions.

In the final stage of the writing of this book, I was struck by the news that she had made a decision on this matter and ended her blogging. Brave and smart. She followed her heart and I am convinced that in the long run she will benefit from it.

can rest during the lesson and can be picked up when it is time for break. There are also schools that are even stricter. Here the younger children may not have their mobiles at all during the entire school day. But many schools have no restrictions. Then it is up to each teacher to set their own limits. Sometimes this leads to an eternal game of cat and mouse. The teacher tells the students to put their phones away, the students do as they are told for a while and then eventually get their phones out again.

Sometimes I see some brilliant exceptions, with students who take digital responsibility. They use their mobiles responsibly, meaning that it does not cause a disturbance. For a mobile is not just social media – it is also a calculator and an encyclopedia.

Mobiles in schools are a constant source of debate. Digital activities are sometimes blamed for declining results at school. The reason is that students lose their ability to concentrate when social media distracts them. The ability to focus more in-depth on tasks can become more difficult for a click and kick-damaged generation. Many students also have private digital activities on the go when they are doing their homework. In the midst of the essay writing, the phone pings and focus is shifted to Snapchat or Instagram. We can see the same phenomenon in adults who, in the middle of their work, suddenly end up in their feed instead of doing their jobs.

Younger children seem to appreciate the calmness that results when the mobiles are not the primary focus. Another point of view is that the children must learn to handle the new technology. It feels reasonable that older teenagers need to learn to take responsibility for themselves. How else will they be able to cope with adult life? At work, there are no online policies that set limits for us adults, we take care of it ourselves.

Having travelled and lectured at various schools, I have noticed an interesting difference between students in the UK and Finland compared to Sweden. In Sweden there were considerably more mobile phones in the students' hands. In the other countries I saw only paper and pens...

It can be a great advantage for schools to create a policy for digital habits in the school environment. Here are some points that students, parents and staff can discuss.

- Should the school have special rules for mobile use? How should these be designed?
- Should the school introduce mobile daycare, total bans or apply freedom of responsibility?
- How should the school handle cyberbullying and bullying?
- Should the staff use private mobiles during working hours and if so, in what way?
- Are there areas where mobiles can be used positively on lessons?

Highly sensitive

Highly Sensitive Personality (HSP) is a personality trait that means that you find it more difficult than others to filter different stimuli. You hear and see everything with greater sharpness and your radar is constantly running.

About 20 percent of all people are HSP, including me. This means that I always check where the life jackets and lifeboats are on a ship. I notice things that others miss. If I am on a bus, I can find it difficult to avert myself from other people's conversations. I find it hard to shut out all kinds of sensory cues; sight, feel, smell, sound and taste.

A person with HSP has a tendency to analyze and dwell on things that others quickly put behind them. When I and other HSP-affected colleagues discussed HSP in connection with social media, I understood that we had experienced similar things; that HSP may result in a greater risk of getting hooked on social media. This is because you notice people's cries for help and feel the need to support everybody. You also want to be there for them and ensure that they feel better.

I think that is why I find it difficult to participate in some Facebook groups, because I feel compelled to comfort, give help and advice.

Do you belong to a risk group?
How do you handle the risk of getting caught?

My 10 best tips for preventing addiction

What can you do to prevent getting hooked on social media? The easiest and only safe thing is to never start. It is possible to live without social media. But if you still want to join the game, here is my best advice:

1   Be wary of how much you use the platforms. If it starts to increase, it is wise to slow down.
2   If you already have free zones where you do not use these platforms, such as the bathroom or bedroom, guard them!
3   If people start to complain about your behaviors, listen to what they have to say without being defensive. They probably just want what's best for you.
4   Make sure to hang out with people you like. In both the digital and analogue forms.
5   Take a digital break every now and then. Do something fun without social media.
6   Exercise your body. It also strengthens your brain and your self-discipline. Try to take a walk without your mobile.
7   Use social media selectively. You should feel that you get some thing positive out of it. Avoid aimlessly zombie scrolling.
8   Only ever use one screen at a time.
9   Avoid conflict with people which doesn't lead anywhere.
10   Do things that are not digital and where you need to focus. Yoga, mindfulness, swimming, climbing or gardening. Nature can be a rich source of relaxation.

6. The digital society

A digital pandemic?

Since 2016, access to the Internet is a human right according to the UN Human Rights Council. This means that governments do not have the legal right to prevent citizens from using the internet. The reason for the decision is that some regimes block and limit internet content for political or ideological reasons. This signal is clear as it shows how the UN considers the internet to be a positive force for popular education and democracy.

Digital technology is getting cheaper and better. The speed of the internet is becoming faster and more stable. Soon, the only areas where there will be digital black spots will be in remote mountain regions. Social media boundaries are practically non-existent. If you have a screen, you can quickly access all the apps in the world. Just by pressing some buttons, I can contact relatives, friends and clients all over the world. This global perspective is one of the great advantages of social media. The internet breaks down walls and is rarely affected by barriers.

At the same time, discussions on the negative effects of social media are taking place all over the world. More and more people in the technology industry, researchers, psychologists, teachers and users talk about the other side of the coin. Everyone testifies to the same thing: that what can begin as a positive use can lead to dependency and addiction. Just as with other addictions, where you live, language, culture and other factors play a minor role. Those who get hooked behave surprisingly similarly, whether they live in Sweden, Canada or Japan. Whilst writing this book, more and more alarming reports have come from all corners of the world.

People are becoming increasingly aware of how social media can create not only positive but also negative effects. The Internet competes with family life, sports, homework and meals. Could it be that social media addiction is part of a digital pandemic? When I discussed the issue with the researcher Mark Griffiths, he emphasized that there are very few nationally representative studies on social media addiction. On the other hand, there are frequent media reports of addiction to mobile phones and social media. It seems that all communities with wide access to digital technology have major problems.

If I combine video game addiction, mobile addiction and social media addiction, it is conceivable that, together, they form the basis for a digital pandemic. As early as 2009, I warned that video game addiction could have had a spread of pandemic preportions. The phenomenon exists throughout much of the world. It is a frightening idea if a large part of the world's population can be exposed to similar problems.

The question of whether social media will be classified as a clinical addiction in the future, is something that dependency researcher Fred Nyberg is very cautious of: "The research provides building blocks that can lead to knowledge later on." I have observed a similar approach with other researchers. The topic needs to be studied more. We had a similar discussion about video game addiction a few years ago, which today is one of the WHO's established diagnoses. Time will tell if we get the same development for social media.

Social resposibility

IT companies earn huge sums and it is you who create their profits. With your time. The business model is based on advertising revenue. The more time you spend on the platforms, the more they earn on the ads. You should bear that in mind when you consider it to be a free service. Your time is other people's money. The question of social responsibility then becomes a paradox. Why would they want you to spend less time on their platforms?

An important question is whether social media providers take enough social responsibility. The companies create a service that, obviously, many find difficult to handle and easy to become addicted to.

A number of former employees at large IT companies have openly warned about what they have caused. They are seriously concerned about the addictive functions they have constructed. Many claims that it is unethical to deliberately create a service that is addictive. We can compare it with soft drinks and energy drinks. If these

My wish list to IT companies for them to take more social responsibility:
- Post a self-test on all platforms that is easy to find and do.
- Provide a clear warning, informing users of the risk of becoming addicted.
- Post tips on healthy online habits.
- Remove the like buttons.
- Increase age limits. Today, most platforms have an age limit of 13-years. But is it really high enough? The parts of the brain that have to do with strategic and long-term thinking are only fully developed at the age of 25.
- Review current business models. Why not do as Spotify: a free advertising service and a pay-per-view service without ads?

contain caffeine, it is likely that people who drink them will become caffeine dependent. Then, consumers are driven to drink more and more because of their dependency, which is beneficial for the producer but can have negative consequences for the consumer.

Mark Zuckerberg has declared that Facebook's stance will follow a Time Well Spent-spirit: that is, to move away from pointless scrolling and focus more on interaction with loved ones. The Time Well Spent movement was founded in California, by former Google associate Tristan Harris. His mission is to be a critical voice against the major technology companies. Harris believes that we should all look at how much time we spend on social media and on our mobiles. I have met the founder of their Swedish branch, Hoa Ly. Hoa is a psychologist and has long been interested in how our online life affects our mental health. He organizes events and raises questions along the same lines as me; that it is not one way or the other. It is about *how* we use the technology. For the sake of yourself and others.

In 2018 something exciting happened. The industry suddenly seemed to take notice of the criticism. In rapid succession, both Apple and Facebook launched new tools to be able to keep track of how much time we spend on digital platforms. Other companies are now following their example at a furious pace. Insurance companies and retail chains are launching campaigns that raise these issues. Whether they are genuinely interested in counteracting addiction or just using a tactic to create goodwill, is difficult to say. But no matter which, it is positive that we can finally talk openly about the other side of the coin.

It is a good thing that technology companies take responsibility for their products, but the question of who will use these services remains. I believe that it is those who are already strongly motivated to change, because those who are hooked will probably need more help.

Another angle is whether these initiatives are really just a way to rid themselves of the responsibility. Like warning signs on cigarette packets. One alternative would be for the companies to work on not creating addictive products to begin with. Is that even reasonable? We couldn't expect a chocolate manufacturer to deliberately launch a disgusting box of chocolates that no one wanted to eat. This is an interesting contradiction, to provide us with exciting products that we want to use while, at the same time, being given the possibility to limit ourselves. Tristan Harris argues that we should not place responsibility on the individual consumer, because the product is addictive. Perhaps a compromise would be best, where both manufacturers and consumers share the responsibility.

Facebook has designed a system for detecting depressed and suicidal users. These users have since been offered various types of support through organizations that work with suicide prevention. This is an excellent example of social responsibility. However, there is an interesting contradiction. What if future research shows a causal link between social media and depression? Then, the IT companies should invest even more in social responsibility and prevent problems from arising in the first place, instead of merely patching up what is already broken.

To find out what some companies think of social responsibility, I contacted a few, and received answers from Facebook and Jodel.

Facebook

As a company, Facebook often wants to present itself as an open and transparent organization. In certain respects, this is certainly true, but there are two professional groups who often disagree. These are investigative journalists and writers.

There are plenty of stories where writers have tried in vain to make contact with representatives of the company. The authors Martin Gelin and Karin Pettersson have visited Facebook's headquarters in Silicon Valley. In their book *Internet är Trasigt* (*The Internet is broken*, translator's note), they wrote that, during visits from journalists, there are strict rules about not talking to employees and that it is forbidden to take photos of desks and computer screens. The fact that a company is concerned about business secrets is nothing strange, but the question is where do you draw the line?

I have sent several email s to the head office and only received standard replies that "we will get back to you". But I have never received an answer. Of course, I have some understanding that a large company cannot provide personal service to everybody who contacts it. But, with Facebook, I have been met with a wall of silence.

The closest I have come to Facebook is their server hall outside the town of Lulea in northern Sweden. Whilst attending a lecture, I took the opportunity to visit the gigantic facility that has been built there for a special reason: the low average temperature that is required to house that much technology. However, the server hall in Lulea is a long way from Facebook's head office in Silicon Valley.

In the absence of a response from the head office, I tried to contact Facebook's office in Stockholm. But getting in touch with the manager in charge was not easy. All contact must be made through their PR agency, which receives questions from the press and authors. I contacted their CEO who, to start with, was very accommodating. At first, it looked as though it might be possible to get an interview with somebody from Facebook's Nordic office. But then they stepped back and asked me to email my questions instead. I wrote down some clear and relevant questions:

- What is your opinion on the fact that many people consider themselves to be addicted to Facebook?
- How would you respond to the criticism that Facebook was designed to be addictive?
- Would you consider creating a platform to prevent addiction?

Their answer didn't really answer my questions. Instead, they quoted a speech that Mark Zuckerberg held in January 2018.

Hi Sven,

Please see below some information about how Facebook works in relation to your questions: Here is an excerpt from a post by Mark Zuckerberg on January 12 this year:

"The research shows that when we use social media to connect with people we care about, it can be good for our well-being. We can feel more connected and less lonely, and that correlates with long term measures of happiness and health. On the other hand, passively reading articles or watching videos – even if they're entertaining or informative – may not be as good.

Based on this, we're making a major change to how we build Facebook. I'm changing the goal I give our product teams from focusing on helping you find relevant content to helping you to have more meaningful social interactions."

/Mark Zuckerberg

Regards,
Anton, Spotlight PR for Facebook in Sweden

Unfortunately, this is common when it comes to Facebook: there is not always the will for dialogue. I was also directed to different links where Facebook expressed social responsibility. From that information, I could start to see hints of the following message: Facebook believes that it is about *how* we use their service. That there is a difference between meaningless scrolling and social contacts with friends. The problem is that they have a business model that is based on the users putting a lot of time into using the service.

What can also be said against Facebook's intentions to take social responsibility is the launch of "Messenger Kids" that is on trial in some countries. It is a service aimed at children under the age of 13. The idea is to meet children's needs for social media. It is a way to enable parents to have more control over the children's online activities. A good thought perhaps, but it has received criticism from children's rights organizations. They believe that children should not be exploited. Children benefit from a reduction in their digital presence, not an increase. I am inclined to agree; I think younger children can benefit from having to wait for access to some digital activities.

As a final attempt at dialogue, I contacted Facebook's Nordic office, via Messenger. This resulted in some pleasant contact via email, Messenger and phone. But my wish for an interview was eventually declined. The reason was that the company, as a principle, did not participate in book projects and that no one in the office was suitable to answer my questions. After that, I requested the name of the person responsible for CSR (Corporate Social Responsibility) with the aim of speaking to the right person. But I got no answer.

Just before this went to print, something happened that could mean a big change: "The future is private." The words caused silence. It was Mark Zuckerberg who, at Facebook's annual conference (F8) in May 2019, declared his and the company's new direction, to focus on the private sphere of the users. The idea is to leave the global perspective, where everyone communicates with each other. The new goal is instead to safeguard the more intimate group of family and close friends. Zuckerberg meant that we should move away from the "digital arena" towards the "digital living room". This was stated as Facebook's new major challenge in the next few years. I interpret this as a serious endeavor. We should bear in mind that the founder of Facebook has developed from a young student into a devoted father. It is normal for life to take on new priorities.

It can also be seen as a sign of the times. Many people today see the value of focusing on their closest friends and family. The big challenge is to find new business models where this is possible, as the quest for users' time is no longer central, and quality comes before aimless scrolling. I think this can be a decisive break from the trend when it comes to some of the risks that I have mentioned in the book. Because when online contacts are characterized by a sense of kinship, it can be perceived as more meaningful. However, critics argue that Facebook, not historically known for caring about personal integrity, is just using empty words. Of course, it remains to be seen whether Zuckerberg will go from words to action. But I'm hopeful.

Jodel
When I emailed the small startup company in Germany, I immediately received a personal response from one of their employees:

• What is your opinion of the fact that many people consider themselves to be addicted to Jodel?
So far, we don't have information that shows us that users are addicted to Jodel. When people used that description in user interviews, we dug deeper and found that they use the term of being addicted to express how much they loved the content and the community. We know that there is a large number of users who like Jodel in that way. So far, we have not heard about addiction to Jodel in the way modern medicine defines it.

• How would you respond to the criticism that social media was designed to be addictive?
Jodel was created to connect people nearby, not to cause addiction. If people can or become addicted, they ultimately don't like the service but are forced to use it because of their addiction. We

don't want that. We want users that don't want to spend a lot of time on Jodel to experience the same value as users who do. We do see services that make use of questionable practices to draw users (mostly younger ones) back into the product but do not believe that these services are initially designed to be addictive.

- Would you consider creating a platform to prevent addiction?
We had several internal discussions about this topic before, as we don't want people to potentially abuse our service. Apple, Google and Instagram are already working on features that help monitor the time spent on mobile/social networks. We are monitoring and discussing these within the company and are constantly revising whether any action from our side would make sense at this point. We are open to help prevent addiction in order to keep our users healthy. Happy to hear your thoughts about this!

Best,
Valentin Oswald + Team Jodel

The major technology companies now seem to be competing to take the greatest social responsibility. Most often by using different ways of measuring your screen time. A good start, perhaps, but is it really the right way forward and is time the most interesting factor? I believe we should be looking more at the sense of meaningfulness. I can have discussions for several hours on my authors' group and feel that I am developing as a writer. But if I spent the corresponding amount of time watching cat videos, I would probably see it as a waste of time.

At the time of writing, Facebook and Instagram have taken this into account. In the spirit of Time Well Spent, we can now set up the way we want to use the services. It is called "digital wellbeing". You can control what comes up in your feed and in what way. Here, the technology companies are on the right track. Not simply looking at the time factor, but also what we do and how it affects us.

Mobiquette

The mobile phone contains more than just social media. There is access to maps, banks, search engines and other useful things. I often see an interplay between "useful" apps and social media, which may require great self-discipline. Often, we automatically click on social media when we check the time or look for directions.

Because many people use social media on their mobiles, the concept of mobile dependency is an interesting one, because even just the fact that we use the mobile, regardless of what we are doing, can have unexpected consequences. In the US and China they have tested the use of warning signs for mobile zombies. On half of the pavement, it is forbidden to use mobile phones – drastic, but perhaps necessary. The reason is that there have been accidents when people have collided whilst looking down at their mobiles. This is a good example of the fact that we have not yet found the ultimate forms of digital interaction in the analogue world.

In my previous book, *Mobikett – handbok för mobilzombies* (*Mobiquette – Handbook for Mobile Zombies*, translator's note), I coined the term mobiquette. This means that we should develop codes of conduct for mobile use. But how do we handle social media when we spend time with other people? Whose rules should apply? Or do we have the right to

An extreme case of mobile addiction is "Snapchat Dysmorphia". It is about patients who have plastic surgery in order to look the way they do on Instagram or Snapchat. Now, patients want a nose as small as they get on Snapchat, but in real life. Crazy, many people say, and I am inclined to agree.

continue with the same mobile behavior that we have when we are alone? There are no obvious answers here, as our terms of reference can be very different, especially between the different user groups. A digital native may consider it perfectly okay to express certain behaviors that a digital immigrant thinks is unacceptable and vice versa. I think the first step is to avoid moralizing and instead try to understand one another. How we handle social media also depends on the context and who we are with. Let me take some typical situations where there may be conflicts.

Imagine a fancy restaurant where there is a group of people about to enjoy a good meal. For many, it is a given to take photos of food and post them on social media, but also to check the mobile during the meal to see what is going on. The consequences can be both cold food and a conversation that is constantly interrupted. Instead, if we give the mobile a rest, the culinary experience becomes more concentrated as our minds focus on the food. Even the conversations will be more pleasant since we don't have to compete with the screens that are being constantly picked up. But of course, it is important to read every situation and adapt to it. During a dinner for two at a fancy restaurant, it may be more important to leave the mobile behind than it would be during an after-work happy hour in a busy tapas bar.

During holidays, the flow on social media usually increases. Many people share everything from beautiful landscapes to restaurant visits. Of course, it may be nice for friends and relatives to see what you are up to, but can it interfere with your experience as a traveler? I think so. If I travel with other people, our interaction may suffer if we constantly stare at our mobile screens. I, myself, have noticed that I have not always been mentally present whilst travelling. Instead, my thoughts have been on how to capture the perfect picture for my followers on Facebook. Nowadays, I try to take pictures during a trip that I then post afterwards. I have noticed how I then become less stressed and more focused in the moment. A bonus effect is that a potential thief doesn't find out that my home is vacant whilst I'm away.

Another aspect is that many people cut themselves off using screens and headphones. A noisy environment can lead to people wanting to shut out the noise, but they then create less opportunities for simple everyday contact with people. At my gym I see the difference clearly; those who shut out external stimuli and train with their own music and those without headphones who can walk around and chat with others. It is not about "right or wrong", but it is clear that mobile use has social consequences for our disengagement in the public space.

The question of mobiquette is particularly important if we are to be able to integrate our digital life into our analogue one. At the end of the day, it is about respect and consideration for our fellow human beings. But also for our own mental health, because if we acquire a balanced approach to our lives online, we also feel better as individuals.

Once, a training partner at the gym had seen my posts on Facebook saying that I was going to take a digital detox. He approached me and asked me whether I had broken the detox now that I was sitting with my phone? But he had misunderstood my aim, he thought the gym would be a completely mobile-free zone for me. My idea was to be without social media, but to still use the mobile to check messages, calendars and other things. This misunderstanding is common. That we often talk about a general mobile addiction, that we are in some way dependent on the actual gadget. I think we have to identify what we are getting hooked on. For me it was social media. For someone else, it may be gambling.

I think it is important to keep in mind that mobiles are used in different ways, in different contexts, by different people with different wills. It is not one-sided, and it would be foolish to put all users into the same bracket. Many see the mobile as a remote control for life. We have calendars, bus tickets and maps in it and it is usually a hub for communication. In this way, it is necessary to have a mobile, just like we would have difficulty coping without electricity.

Are you addicted to your mobile?
Do you think you have good mobiquette?

What is okay to post?

The attitude on social media can be both cruel and harsh. Many people still perceive that what is happening online is not real, but for those who suffer from net hate, it is usually worse than if it had happened in the analogue, as it can spread like a never-ending online tsunami.

Fortunately, our legal system is beginning to catch up. There are several cases where people have been convicted of online abuse. I think it is important that we realize that what is happening online is very much part of our modern reality.

Is it okay to post whatever you like on social media? No, I believe that we must take others into account and have reasonable limits to what we post.

Some areas where we should be careful are:
• Pictures of young children, especially naked. There is a risk that they will spread among pedophiles and the child has not been able to choose whether or not to appear on the internet. In order to safeguard personal integrity, it is reasonable that each and every individual decides for themselves what is posted about them.
• Semi-naked images. It is difficult to know where to draw the

line, and we also have different views on nudity in different cultures. But many young people are easily triggered to show off more than what they really want.

- People who do not want to be photographed and posted. Today there seems to be a new norm where we assume that it is always okay to photograph and post pictures of others. I think we should be more considerate and actually ask the person it affects.
- Sexism and gender discrimination are not okay.
- Racism, incitement against certain groups and threats.
- Insults. A kind attitude benefit everybody.

Think twice before you post anything. If you are in doubt, it is best to delete than to post.

Have you ever been treated badly on social media?
If so, how did you react?
Do you ever reflect on what you are posting?

Social media at work

If we go back to the time before the digital revolution, our working lives were very different. I remember the only times when it was okay to take a break were during coffee breaks, lunch breaks or when you needed to use the bathroom. How does our work ethic look today?

Most people take their private mobiles to work. This applies to everybody from teachers to shop staff. In many workplaces, there is no policy for private mobile use, and it is up to each individual to take responsibility for themselves so that their mobiles do not interfere with their work. When I walk past offices, I enjoy observing people's work discipline. It is common to see both Facebook and Instagram on the computer screens. Or that the mobile phone is taking priority over the work computer.

These days, employers are worried that private internet use takes up too much work time. I read a study that showed that as much as 17.5 percent of working hours were spent on private surfing. That means a total of almost a whole day a week. On the other hand, there are many who reply to work emails after working hours. Then it is about give and take.

Of course, there is a difference between different industries in how this affects the workplace and customer relationships. I would find it irritating to be met by a shop assistant who looked at their mobile when I needed their help. It shows me that the staff member has made themselves unavailable and has no interest in the customer. On the other hand, I don't mind if someone is sitting in a ticket booth in the subway and checking their mobile when they have no work to do. But staff at a retirement home cannot feed a patient with one hand and check their mobile with the other. Mobile use at work is determined by the situation.

Of course, sliding between work and private life can work painlessly, but to have a clear policy is often better for all parties. More and more companies are adopting digital policies, but in many workplaces, it is still up to the employee and the manager to do what they think is best.

If you want to create a discussion about this at your job, you might find the questions on the following page useful.

Policy in the workplace

I believe that employers should have a policy on how staff are allowed to use digital technology for private purposes. Below are suggestions of questions to discuss in the workplace:

1. Apart from during breaks, may the employee use their computer and mobile for private purposes? This includes all types of private activity, i.e. conversations, text messages, playing games and being active on social media.

2. Is it okay for employees to discuss their work on private social media accounts?

3. Can the employee be encouraged to have a special professional profile on social media for work purposes, such as School Nurse Anna, in order to be available to students during school hours?

4. Are staff expected to respond to work email and text messages after working hours?

5. Is there an opportunity to get a separate work mobile to more easily keep working hours and leisure apart?

6. If employees have direct customer contacts, what are the rules for private mobile use?

Social media as a profession

To get the opinion of someone who uses social media in their profession, I met with the social media personality and actor Toni Prince Tvrtkovic. He is one of the people behind the Instagram success @sprakforalla ("language for all", translator's note). They have almost half a million followers and display humor, often featuring cultural clashes. Toni originally dreamt of becoming a professional footballer, but the success that came with @sprakforalla has opened new doors. Now Toni is trying out a career as an artist and actor.

On the question of pressure to be active on social media, Toni believes that it is he himself that sets the bar for how often he should post. He is aware that there is a risk that the pressure will get too high.

Toni believes that Instagram is the most addictive platform of them all. The reason for this is the enormous amount of material that is posted and that many people have difficulty in not checking their feeds.

When we talk about exercise, Toni says that he tries to avoid social media. He prefers to focus on his training. But he is happy to listen to music through his mobile and can film himself in order to study his technique.

Toni believes that we need to take the warning signs of too much mobile use seriously. Headache, eye strain and stress are signs of unnatural behavior – an addiction. At the same time, he does not want us to completely stop using modern technology. I understand, social media is his livelihood. He believes that digital balance can be created, but he thinks that the major technology companies should take more social responsibility. If it escalates, the development can be devastating to humanity because we risk losing focus on what is important in life.

Just like many other people, Toni is becoming tired of aimless scrolling. He wants more focus on what is meaningful. He tries to start the day quietly, without a mobile. He reads books and loves listening to classical music. He thinks that education is important and not just the superficial knowledge that one gets on social media.

When he talks to his peers about easing off on their mobile phone usage, some of them say, "Am I supposed to just stare at the wall then, if I can't use my mobile?" He sees this as a clear defense of an addiction. Just like a drug addict who always says: "I'll give it up soon." And when Toni asks his friends what they would take with them if they were stranded on a desert island, the answer is often: the mobile!

Toni believes that we need to invest more in socializing than just hanging around on Instagram. Those who have read too many books do not get addiction problems like those who play too many video games or use social media. Books do not make us depressed or hooked.

After taking some photos of Toni and saying goodbye, I started to think. Here is a representative of the online generation who is warning about the developmental issues associated with social media, even though it is his livelihood. We should listen to him.

7. Creating digital balance

You become your choices

Let's start by making it clear that you have the opportunity to choose. Either you can decide for yourself what your digital life should look like, or you can follow the stream like a dead fish. Despite this, many people think it is impossible to choose, that peer pressure pushes us in a certain direction. To a large extent, this applies to our presence on social media. If the majority of a school class uses Snapchat, it may be almost impossible for an individual student to not join them. Even adults can feel a peer pressure around social media. Many invitations to parties and events take place through Facebook and if you are not involved you may be forgotten.

You should consider what you really want. Join in. Or don't. And in what way. Because it is not predetermined. You should be the one in control, not the managers on Facebook or Snapchat. Here is an interesting question if you believe in free will. What happens to our will if it is occupied by an addiction? Especially if those who create that addiction earn huge amount of money from it. Can we hand the responsibility over to technology companies? Or the authorities? I believe that everyone has a huge personal responsibility. At least adults. But on the other hand, technology companies should help us make these choices. I will return to this important issue in the chapter on social responsibility.

What do you think of free will when it comes to social media? Are you the one who decides how to use the platforms?

If we get hooked

When I quit smoking, I made a decision. I had tried to just stick to social smoking on special occasions, but each time I returned to being chain-smoker. After some thought, I realized that for me it was either or. Intermittent periods of moderate smoking simply didn't work. I understood that I needed to quit smoking altogether – not even another drag, and the goal was to be smoke-free forever. One day at a time. That was what eventually made me stop smoking.

An old truth is that if a person is trapped in an addiction, it is difficult to switch this to just being a user. An alcoholic or nicotine addict must stop completely, or they will continue their addiction. Does the same then apply to digital abuse? Do I have to put Facebook aside for good if I'm hooked? Can I never send a Snap, or post a photo on Instagram again?

As these addictions are new, there are no obvious answers yet. However, we can speculate and try different solutions. Let's compare with some other types of abuse.

Imagine a person who has had problems with their eating. They eat so much unhealthy food that they become seriously obese. High blood pressure, diabetes and premature death are becoming realistic scenarios. But the person cannot stop eating altogether. If they did, they would die. The goal must be to achieve a balanced diet.

An even closer example is video game addiction. When I help clients hooked in the world of gaming, I encourage them choose their goal: Stop playing altogether or create balance. Most choose to try to create balance. There has been a wide difference in solutions. Some have opted out of their main problem game, that which they played the most and never managed to control. Instead, they have found new games that enable them to play sensibly. One case was a young man who had spent 50 hours a week playing World of Warcraft. His studies, health and family life had crashed. Nowadays he just occasionally plays the Rocket League; a simple and fast game that is different to the game he has been dependent on. This journey took a few years but is a good example of the fact that it is possible to reverse the cycle.

I believe that people hooked on social media have the same opportunity, to achieve balance instead of stopping altogether.

How to break free

How can you break free if you are hooked on social media? In my opinion, it is wise to have a large selection of alternative methods. We humans work differently and sometimes need different solutions for the same problem. To just point in one direction is too simplistic, I rarely believe in clear-cut solutions to human problems.

Here are a number of different ways to achieve digital balance. I hope you find a path that suits you. Remember that you may be able to find your own model to move forward.

Focus on one screen

Availability controls the risk of misusing something. High availability provides greater risks than if you have some kind of restrictions. This applies to alcohol, sweets and, above all, social media. Personally, I only use social media on my mobile, not on my laptop, tablet or desktop computer. When I use my computer, I can put my mobile away and therefore not be disturbed by social media. Some people do the opposite, they remove the apps from the mobile and are only active on their computer. Whatever you choose, it can create a comfortable restriction not to be active on all screens.

When I discuss social media with others, the issue of mobiles often comes up. For mobile phones give the option of being active on social media whenever and wherever. For better or worse. The question is whether we always need to have all the social media apps on our mobiles?

I spoke to a barista about this. Rino owns a small coffee shop in Stockholm. He runs the café with his wife, and they are busy all day, every day. A few years ago, Rino noticed that he was checking Instagram in his café and almost missed a customer. Then he made a drastic decision. He took away all the social media apps from the mobile and just logged in on his computer when he came home in the evening. He immediately felt a relief when he withdrew control. Now he could concentrate on the work he loves; making perfect coffee and talking to customers.

Technical aids

We easily get hooked on digital technology. But the same technology can also create opportunities to help us.

These days, there is an increasing number of technical aids to help you gain control of your digital life. For example, you can let apps measure how much you use other apps. You can then get an overview of how you use your mobile. The risk is, however, that you can get caught up in new digital technology, that you become addicted to a new app to regulate another app. Therefore, controls that are built directly into Facebook, for example, are good. Then no new app is needed.

Most social media apps now include an opportunity to count how much time you spend on that particular platform. You can also set a ration for how much you want to use the platform. Although time does not tell us everything, I know that a lot of people appreciate this opportunity. It is like a reverse step counter, where you can get a wake-up call if your numbers are too high. Especially if you have had the feeling that social media takes time from other things that you would rather prioritize.

Take a break

Having longer or shorter breaks from social media is becoming increasingly popular. I often see posts in my feed where a friend says "I am now logging out for the weekend". If you are stuck in a certain behavior, there are many benefits to taking a break. Your brain gets a rest and you are able detect any withdrawal symptoms. During a break you can see how you react. Are you stressed out and have difficulty concentrating? Do you get a strong desire to go back? Do you get stress symptoms such as headache, increased heart rate or high blood pressure?

If you experience symptoms of abstinence, it may be good to find something that distracts you. Take a walk or a coffee break with a

I met a person on a train journey that told me something interesting. She had thought that social media took too much time, so she decided to just check her Instagram feed once a week. She worked in another town and took the opportunity when she was on the train. For five hours she went through everything that had happened. I noticed how she got stressed out because I was bothering her, she saw her checking of Instagram on the train as something important, like a duty not to be missed. Of course, I respected her need for silence and instead worked on this script.

good friend. The advantage of the occasional break is that you put some distance between you and the social media. It will not be the most important thing in your life, and you will realize that you can survive without your feed. You may even find other activities that enrich your life.

Screening

When I was most attached to social media, I sometimes thought about logging out for good, as I did with smoking many years ago. But I thought that I could test a softer path first by screening my feeds. Social media can easily become a routine, that you follow the same people and pages as you have always done, instead of making conscious choices.

When you screen, you select the platforms that are most problematic for you. You then focus on one or a few others. I have talked to several people who have left Facebook to focus on Instagram instead. Or vice versa.

Another way of screening is *within* a platform. Which people and pages should you follow? Which groups do you really want to participate in? Let your interest and what makes you feel good be the guide.

Instagram – digital methadone?

If I were to give advice to an alcoholic it would be to stop drinking completely. I would not just advise them to change the type of alcohol. "Try vodka if you drink too much whiskey. Or a Spanish wine instead of Italian." It is the substance alcohol we become addicted to.

However, a change can work when it comes to social media. I've talked to a number of people hooked on Facebook. They think that it takes too much time and they become stressed. A solution has then been to end their Facebook account but still use Instagram. They find that Instagram is easier to manage in less time. We don't get stuck in long discussions or end up somewhere else by clicking on links.

I would like to compare Instagram with methadone, the opiate derivative that can replace heroin and enable an addict to have a functioning life. Similarly, Instagram seems to give an opportunity for a quieter life on social media. Today, it is so widespread that, socially, there is hardly any shortfall. You can still keep in touch with friends and acquaintances.

Of course, even Instagram can become problematic for some people and then a switch to Facebook, Twitter or Snapchat can work. My point is, try to identify which platform you find most difficult to handle and test an alternative.

Mobile daycare and mobile hotels

Another solution is to leave your mobile phone in a mobile daycare or mobile hotel. In schools this has been around for a while, but similar systems are now appearing in restaurants and concerts. The idea is that you should not have to think about your self-discipline, but you let somebody else look after your mobile.

One company has even started with replacement phones. When you hand in your smartphone you will be able to borrow a simpler model to be able to call and text. This can be found, as an example, at a large mountain resort in Sweden where the idea is that you should be able to focus on your mountain holiday without any digital disturbance. Similar offers are now appearing at travel agencies that market analogue beach holidays, without digital technology.

A more basic mobile

One alternative is to buy a simpler type of mobile, not a smartphone, which you can only call and text with. Then you can only use social media when sitting at another screen. It is a drastic type of rationing but perhaps worth testing. I, myself, have tried this by dusting off an older mobile. However, I quickly noticed that my everyday life became more complicated. The reason is that I also have utility apps in my mobile that simplify my everyday life. But sometimes I meet people who think this is a perfect solution.

Therapy

Talking to a psychologist or counsellor is very helpful for many people when life gets difficult. It has become increasingly common for us to turn to an expert for guidance. It can be about everything from how we feel psychologically to relationships with others. It is a feeling of indulgence to have a professional person focusing on our problems.

If you are at school, you will most likely have access to a counsellor or psychologist. This can be a good start point for conversations. As an adult, you are able to receive therapy through your health center or private clinic. Today, more and more health centers are starting to work with digital abuse. In cases where a social media abuse is an escape, talking to someone can be especially important. An investigation can then help you get to the bottom of your problems.

Self-help groups

Paradoxically, Facebook can also support you if you get hooked on social media. There are many groups based on the idea of peer support, where people with similar problems support and help each other. It's free and more informal than professional help. Social media is constantly open so you can get immediate answers to your questions. I therefore see it as a good complement to other support. I have started the Facebook group Scrollzombies where you are welcome to discuss and receive support. Just watch out so you don't get hooked there...

Digital detox centers and treatment centers

An old method of breaking an addiction is to travel. Even a hundred years ago, "bad lads" could go to sea or join the Army. The idea was to remove them from their old environment and leave their problems behind. Since then, various types of treatment homes and detox camps have been built up. This may apply to classic dependency problems such as alcohol but also to modern, digital abuse.

Here are two types. The longer-term treatment homes where you live and remain for a longer period. These usually apply to younger people who have a mixed screen misuse surrounding games and social media. There are also shorter varieties of detox camps. They mainly target adults who want to take a short break from their digital life.

I have had an exciting meeting with Karina DiLucia, who runs a digital detox center in northern Sweden. When you check in, you leave all your digital technology locked in a cabinet. The idea is that for a few days you will be offline.

You walk, eat and talk in beautiful and calm surroundings. Completely without digital interference. Karina welcomes adults who go there voluntarily. Guests seem satisfied with their stay and perceive a calm that they have not known for a long time. Karina's services are increasingly in demand, which shows that more and more people are experiencing a digital stress.

What appeals to me with her approach is its simplicity. Being in beautiful surroundings and enjoying walks and good food, without demonizing the problems of mobile use. The idea is to be able to go back to a more harmonious use after having received some insights from the stay.

You can also arrange something similar yourself. I usually have a mini-detox where I prioritize kayaking and fishing above my life online. A rest from the hubbub of the digital world is important to the modern person.

Log out from social media

A drastic alternative is to log out completely from social media. You might miss out on some things, but you will also experience great freedom. More and more people are making this decision. Even more people seem to consider it, but hesitate because they feel anxiety about how they will manage without social media. They do not want to miss the positive effects they get from it. Some of those who log out come back later. They realize that the benefits of smooth communication can be difficult to replace in an analogue fashion.

If you are considering logging out, you can make a list of pros and cons. You should initially determine the time perspective; you can log out for a limited period of time and see how it goes. But you can also do as I did when I quit smoking; be definitive and think in terms of "never again". Again, I want to emphasize your opportunity to choose. It's your life and your choices. Keep in mind that if you log out, it is always possible to come back.

Several well-known people in recent years have chosen to back away from social media. One example is actress Alicia Vikander, who left Instagram in March 2018. She felt pressurized to constantly post pictures. Whether or not she will come back, nobody knows.

5-step digital balance program

I will now describe a program that I created to cure my own social media addiction. It consists of 5 steps where each step takes a week to complete. I suggest you write a logbook of your experiences, preferably every day but at least once a week. This way, you can track your progress and see where your problem areas are.

Step 1: Observe your behavior

Start the program by using social media as usual. Take notes on what you do and what you experience. Include both positive and negative things, preferably situations where social media collides with other things.

Step 2: Self-test and free zones

Before you begin step two, you should do a self-test. Answer yes or no and be honest in your answers, otherwise you will just fool yourself. Use your notes from step 1 to see how your usage really looks, not how you *think* or *believe* it looks. Try to make connections. Note that it is only a self-test, which only gives an indication of your situation, not a professional statement.

Once you have done the test, try to embrace the result. Please tell someone you trust: a partner, sibling, friend or workmate. Then you can get support in your process.

For the rest of the week, you should have at least three zones free of social media, places where you would normally use social media.

Then write a list of the positive and negative effects of social media – what consequences do you think they have for you?

The last thing to do is to formulate a clear goal. For example, you can choose one of these goals, or come up with your own:

    A. I will stop completely with social media.
    B. I am going to change how I use social media and create a digital balance.

Step 3: Look but don't act

Now you should just try to check your social media but without posting, sharing, liking or commenting yourself. A new routine is to switch off your mobile phone one hour before you go to bed.

Self-test

■ Do you usually feel compelled to use social media?

■ Do you get a bad conscience if you do not like something that a friend has posted?

■ Do you ever get disturbed by social media when you are studying or working?

■ Have friends, family or others complained about how much you use social media?

■ Are you more active today on social media than a year ago?

■ If you do not have access to social media, does it make you feel stressed?

■ Are you active on social media while exercising?

■ Are you active on social media when eating meals with family or friends?

■ Do you use social media while driving a car, boat, motorcycle or bicycle?

■ Do you see social media the first thing you do when you wake up?

■ Are you using social media in bed before going to sleep?

■ When you see something beautiful, remarkable or unusual, do you first and foremost think about posting it on social media?

■ Are you active on social media while on the toilet?

■ Have you thought about leaving social media?

■ Do you ever use social media instead of doing something else that you should do?

■ Have you tried to reduce or leave social media but fallen back into the old patterns?

NUMBER OF YES-ANSWERS:

0–5: GREEN ZONE
You seem to have control. Continue as you do today.

6–9: YELLOW ZONE
You seem to have several warning signs. Maybe time to step down a bit?

10–16: RED ZONE
You seem to be hooked. Time to stop and think about new habits. Maybe try a digital detox?

Step 4: A total detox

Now comes the biggest challenge of the program. During this week you will be completely free from all social media. One hundred percent. This means that you neither check, share, post, like or comment. Write a diary about how you feel and what happens.

Step 5: Learn

Now is the time to learn and decide how your life on social media will look. You can choose to step back into the community if you wish. But you should only choose the platforms that you missed in a positive way. In this step you also need to screen groups and friends/contacts. Remove everything that you feel is just wasting time and doesn't give you anything back. You should also decide whether to keep any free zones. The path towards digital balance is based on you making active choices.

My top tips for creating digital balance

For those of you who want to remain on social media, there is only one solution. To achieve digital balance. To regain control. Here are my top tips for achieving balance.

1. Remember that you are the one making the choices. Try to ignore peer pressure and the sense of "having to".
2. Focus on one, or a maximum of three, platforms. You don't have to be everywhere.
3. If you have trouble putting your mobile down: remove the apps from it. Just check them when you are at your computer.
4. Take the occasional break. One hour. One day. One week. Whatever works for you.

5. Select some zones where you avoid social media. It can be the breakfast table, the bedroom or the sofa.
6. Remove notifications, banners and other disturbances that cause your cell phone to attract your attention.
7. Try setting time limits for your social media apps.
8. Ration what you post. Not everything you post is interesting to everybody else.
9. If certain apps cause a problem, make them difficult to reach. For example, don't have them on the home page of your screen where you will see them as soon as you unlock your mobile.
10. Exercise your body and spend time outside, without digital technology. It sharpens your brain and gives you a much-needed mental rest.

8. Conclusion

We still live in the midst of a digital revolution. The speed of technological development is faster than our analogue brains can keep pace with. This is especially true of social media. We must bear in mind that our socializing on Facebook is just over ten years old. Yet we take our digital life as a matter of course, as if it has always existed and will always be there.

How will our lives on social media develop? Although a certain resistance movement is in progress, it is hardly likely that social media will decrease in scope. Rather, I think the platforms will be developed and that new smart apps will increase our presence. VR technology will captivate us by making the experience on social media more and more authentic. The boundaries of what is real and not will become blurred and the distances between people will reduce.

Facebook Spaces is a newly launched VR app where you can interact with Facebook friends through a VR device. The technology is already here. Our connected lives will soon be even faster and smoother than today. Everything will feel like a given (much like older technology that we take for granted today) when the paradigm shift is over, and the digital revolution prevails.

But what of the resistance movement? These days, we can see that people choose to go offline, for shorter or longer periods. Digital stress means that many people perceive relief in having a digital detox.

Will we succeed in solving our digital dependence? Will we see even worse school results in the future? Or are we developing a new type of human. A person who has a more fragmented approach. Someone who does a little work here and a little work there, without being able to focus for longer periods, but who can cope with constant interruptions and still come back. I hope that, in the future, we will find solutions without us having to sacrifice a whole generation.

I think we all need to help each other out. Both parents and children, technology companies and psychologists, staff in school and health care. We all have an important job to do in the quest for a common digital balance.

I hope you enjoyed my book. My aim was to highlight several perspectives on social media. Both the positive and the things that cause problems. Social media has a bit of everything. Love and hate. Friendship and conflicts. Good and Evil. Generosity and meanness. Just like in our other lives. Life on social media is rarely black or white – it is full of exciting grey areas where the answer often becomes "it depends" instead of yes or no.

Towards the end of writing this book, I sometimes considered logging out for good. More and more, I get the feeling of having been coerced into something. A niggling feeling of not being in control. It is one of several reasons why I believe that social media addiction exists. But the important thing is that it is possible to handle and regain control. For those who want to close your accounts, it is also a possibility. Personally, I will keep struggling to achieve digital balance. Whichever way *you* choose, I hope you find a path that suits you. The choice is yours.

FAQ

Over the years, I have received many relevant questions about social media. Here is a selection:

My wife is manic with Facebook and Instagram. She takes pictures everywhere and always has her mobile in her hand. On the sofa in front of the TV, at dinner and during our holidays. I only use LinkedIn. She calls me a Facebook freeloader whenever I ask how a friend or relative is doing. We are constantly arguing about this and I wonder what is the best way to handle it?

What you describe is common, that one party in a relationship is less digitally active. There are a few simple things you can do to reduce your conflicts. Determine some mobile-free zones where nobody uses their mobile. For example, during meals and when watching TV. Negotiate and try to compromise. You will both benefit from it.

My daughter drives me crazy. She is obsessed with social media. She can hardly do anything without checking her phone. Her homework suffers and she lies with her mobile in bed when she should be sleeping. When I tell her, she gets angry. What should I do?

I think you should set some rules. That she does her homework without her mobile and that she does not keep her mobile phone in her bedroom. Explain that it is for her own sake.

My 10-year-old son wants to use social media, but it has a higher age limit. He says that all his friends of the same age are allowed by their parents. How should I handle this?

The age rules should be seen as a recommendation for the reason that younger children may have more difficulty in managing conflicts that could arise and understanding all the content that is posted. I do not think there is any hurry for him to be connected. Also, check with other parents if it is true that their children are allowed to use social media. The argument "everyone else is allowed" is not always true.

My older sister is posting pictures of me that I don't like. When I tell her, she ignores me and carries on. I get annoyed but don't know what to do.

I think everyone has the right to say no to something being posted on social media. Stand up for yourself and talk to your parents. Perhaps you should sit together with the whole family and talk through what rules should apply.

My dad uses social media pretty much all the time. When I tell him, he just gets angry. I'm starting to get tired of it and don't know what to do.

If you have another adult at home, all three of you could talk together. Explain, in a positive way, that you want better contact with your dad. One trick is to use the same platform and communicate this way.

I work as a teacher and am tired of the students using Instagram and Snapchat during my lessons. Telling them off takes both time and energy. But they pick up their phones as soon as I turn my back. What should I do?

Arguing about mobiles in school is common. Many schools choose to have mobile-free lessons. This is where all the mobiles are put in a box – a mobile daycare – and can be collected after the lesson. Another solution is that the mobiles can be put in the students' lockers or schoolbags. This will create a much calmer atmosphere. If your school does not want to be as strict, it is still important to have a clear policy on what does apply.

I have an employee who is always staring at his mobile phone, even if a customer comes into the shop. I have tried to explain that this is not okay, but he ignores me and says that he has the right to have a mobile at work.

You can absolutely demand that the staff focus on their jobs during working hours. A practical solution may be to introduce breaks when the staff can use the mobile for private matters.

Bonuschapter: How I got hooked online and created digital balance

This part of the book is about my own, very personal, journey, about how I got caught in a social media addiction. And how I managed to escape.

Using the internet, computers and mobiles has been a natural part of my life since the early 90's. I saw the benefits of digital technology early on and have never longed to return to the days of typewriters and faxes. Despite this, I always start a new book project with pen and paper. It gives a wonderful physical feeling and helps me to not slide onto the internet. Because I can admit that I often become absorbed in the digital world.

I was a late-starter with Facebook. At first, I didn't really understand the point of spending so much time in this "pretend life". And to display my private life on the internet? No, I gladly abstained from it. But in the autumn of 2009, I was sitting at my computer and creating an account. This means that I had been outside of Facebook since the Swedish launch in 2006. Was it three lost years or a healthy skeptical attitude? That's the question. With support from one of my children I was up and running. Now it was about quickly adding friends, because it felt sad to be alone on this already gigantic platform.

There are various reasons why we start using social media. For me it was mainly that I was curious about what many of my friends were talking about. I felt left out. My argument that it was pointless and silly no longer held. So many users could not possibly be wrong. The fact that I am a social person also had great importance, because I realized that there was a fantastic opportunity to connect with both old and new acquaintances. My work with the negative side of our digital lives was also a driving force. Just like when I felt compelled to start playing games to understand video game addiction. It was out of respect for my clients that I entered into in this world and not just view it from the outside.

How I noticed I was hooked

"It's time for dinner, Sven," said my partner with a cheerful voice.

"I'm coming, I'm just doing something first."

"Okay."

Five minutes later: "Are you coming down?"

"Sure, in a minute."

This went on for at least fifteen minutes, then my partner got fed up and came and checked what was going on.

"Ah, are you sitting at the computer again? Your food is getting cold," she said, now noticeably irritated.

This is my first memory of how I got hooked online. It was many years ago and I was taking a course in SCUBA diving. I had found a dive forum online. It was a popular site and I was learning a lot and having fun. When my partner interrupted me, I was in the middle of an important discussion. That is how it felt. As she had interrupted something important.

I had posted a comment about reserve air during diving and the debate became lively. Since I was the one who started the thread, I felt a responsibility to answer questions. Every night I sat at the computer and read, wrote posts and had discussions. It felt both meaningful, fun and social. Almost as if for real – but online.

Six months earlier, I had questioned a relative's constant presence on a dog-forum. How could she be so active on the internet and talk about dogs? Now I was sitting there myself. Every night. I often got stuck and dinner times had to wait. The discussion on the dive forum could not wait. This was a time when smartphones were still in their infancy and I sat mainly at home on my desktop every evening.

Many years later, a similar event took place. The big difference was that smart phones had created the opportunity to be connected everywhere and at any time. We were eating dinner one sunny summer's day and suddenly my mobile was in my hand. Something had happened on Facebook. When my family asked what I was doing, my answer was: "Erm, I'm just checking an important work email." I lied because I didn't want to tell the truth; that a discussion on Facebook felt more important than being with my family. It was then that I realized that I was really hooked, that I had lost control of my Facebook use. Because I had lied to my family. Lies are a common warning sign of an addiction. I knew that. The lie became like a fog to hide my addiction.

A few weeks later I am taking part in an interview on morning TV, about to talk about digital balance during the summer holidays. How children and adults would be able to combine an active summer with online games and social media. Suddenly I noticed how I told the story about my lie. The TV presenters went quiet. In the end, they realized that I was not joking, and I felt a deep sense of relief. Now I had confessed the truth to the entire population of Sweden. I was hooked on Facebook. Now the question was how I would break free.

All in

When I decided to write this book, I made a conscious and decisive choice. I would conduct some personal research by maximizing my life on social media. My goal was to be as active as possible. Just like the journalist who was practically eating himself to death on fast food in, what became, the documentary film "Super-Size Me".

My focus was Facebook and Jodel. My plan was to over-consume the apps and observe myself. I joined a huge amount of Facebook groups, about cats, writing, exercising, hiking, social work and took every opportunity to discuss things with people. Preferably on topics that I knew would generate debate.

My family soon began to complain. They felt I was always on the phone. During meals, trips and when watching TV. At first, everything went according to plan, but what started as an experiment ended with an addiction. I got hooked on social media. If I am honest, I was probably already there, but I went from a light risk-use to an addiction. I slid from the yellow zone to the red.

A few years earlier, I had used the same research method when I wrote my book about video game addiction. I started playing a lot of games and noticed that I was increasingly drawn into the gaming world. My solution was to quit online games and just partake in single player games, to play offline without contact with other people, which is often easier to handle. I could decide for myself how long I would play and not depend on others, and no one else was dependent on me. It is a solution that I still give as advice to clients.

Was it possible to do something similar with social media? Would I be able to use the services in a balanced way? That was my next big challenge.

When one of my adult children challenged me to take a break from Facebook, I said that I couldn't, because of my research. It was a typical sign of how I defended my addiction, only then I didn't realize it.

All these groups

I can see a clear turning point in my life on social media. It was when I joined my first Facebook group. After that, I spent more and more time online. Sometimes I wonder if my dependence has largely been about these groups. In groups I can get advice and encouragement about my writing, how I should service my boat engine and get tips on new social work methodology. Often, debates arise that are impossible to leave, and I can spend ages in discussion, because everyone wants to continue talking – even if it clashes with other things. Why should we have different rules and etiquette in the digital world? If I stand talking to someone in the street, I would hardly leave in the middle of a discussion, would I?

I have been involved in a few groups that I have been blocked from. The reasons were extremely unclear. Was I rude? Was I threatening? Was I sexist? Not at all. So, what happened then? Well, I was subjected to the phenomenon "groupthink", where there is a refusal to accept anyone who has a different opinion. In one group, I had asked a question about the scientific evidence for a particular discussion. A fairly reasonable question in the 21st century, you might think. But apparently the evidence did not exist, which immediately led to a massive backlash towards me that ended with me being blocked. Is this phenomenon something that is typical of social media? Probably not. We often see the same thing in political parties, associations and sports clubs. Humans often behave like pack animals preferring to be with like-minded people.

In some groups I have also encountered poor leadership. In such cases, it has seemed as though the administrators have behaved like power-hungry psychopaths. They block members on questionable grounds and shut down threads for dubious reasons. I have often heard complaints from other members about the same phenomenon. Therefore, new groups appear, covering the same subjects. People get fed up and try to start their own groups with a more open and honest attitude.

I realize that those who start and run groups on Facebook sometimes lack the experience of leadership. Many do the best they can as it is often something that they do voluntarily, during their leisure time. Obviously, poor leadership can also be found outside of Facebook groups. Managers who are poor leaders, parents and teachers who are not good role models or who act unpredictably.

Fortunately, there is no obligation to join these groups. My solution is to only be in groups that have a positive atmosphere with a high level of acceptance. Because there are countless groups to choose from online.

Another aspect of online forums is that they can attract troublemakers. I have observed people who are constantly looking to pick a fight. It can be anything from poor grammar to which one is the best tent for camping. The subject itself seems, to some, to take second place; the goal is the heated discussion. It is reminiscent of people I sometimes encounter in the public space, those who always find something that annoys them in order to create a conflict, whether it is about how to behave in a bus queue or the issue of disruptive mobile phones. These people are probably not happy, and my attitude is usually a low-arousal approach. I avoid being provoked and would rather back-off than get caught up in a never-ending discussion.

I, myself, have started groups concerning social work, as well as a cat group for fellow social workers. It started out as a fun discussion in a general group for social workers. It was a member who, for fun, had started *Social workers who like heavy metal music*. He wondered which other subgroups could be started. Since I am a doer, I started the group *Social workers who like cats* and we quickly got hundreds of members. It is probably Facebook's most amusing group. Here we post pictures and movies of our cats. There are never any fractions or poisonous discussions. Only love! It is a good example of what social media can also mean. A place to refuel positive energy.

5 steps towards digital balance

Once I had realized that I was hooked, I decided to change. I used all of my accumulated experience as an addiction expert and constructed a simple-to-follow five-step program. Each step took a week to complete. The plan was to gradually slow down and to slowly get used to a different form of digital life.

My motivation was strong, because I was tired of not being in control. I liked social media, but I was not comfortable with how it governed my life. Since I perceive social media in itself to be something positive, my goal has been to create balance and not to log out completely.

Step 1 – Observing my behavior

I started the program using social media as usual. I wrote notes on what I did and how it felt. I also began to reflect on my behavior, which I had not done much of before.

Monday: Jodel: Laughed at childish jokes. Voted down racist and sexist posts. It felt good.

Facebook: Discussion in an author group and a social workers' group. Wished friends a happy birthday.

Instagram: As usual, some general scrolling and liking. I check more than I post and don't follow that many accounts.

Tuesday: Facebook: It's national cream cake day and I posted a picture of a cream cake. Chatted to a friend who was travelling in Thailand. He seems to be enjoying the warm weather whilst I am in the middle of rainy Stockholm. A bit jealous.

Commented on Jocke's speech about screen time and the mobile ban in schools.

I found a funny cat video that I shared. It was of a cat gently playing with a bird.

Seems to be a lively discussion about ADHD in school. It started with a question about boring children's books. As often happens, the discussions slipped into something else. Unfortunately, a calm discussion sometimes turns into a veritable war of words. Where no one gives in.

The feed on Jodel was dominated by cream cakes and the ongoing terrorist trial. Highs and lows. Typical Jodel. I have a real love/hate relationship with that platform. Smart young people, discussing everything with no filters.

Wednesday–Thursday: A bit of Facebook and Jodel. Nothing special.

Friday–Sunday: Went away on a writing weekend in the archipelago. Active on Facebook. Jodel, as usual, is completely dead out on the island.

Step 2 – Self-test och free zones
I started the week by doing the self-test. I got a full house.

Benefits with social media

+ I can keep in touch with people I do not meet very often.
+ Good dialogue with clients.
+ I can learn more about things, such as authorship.
+ It is an easy-going and fun pastime.
+ If I am alone, I can still have rewarding social relationships.

Disadvantages with social media

- It takes time and disrupts me when I do other things: writing, exercising, cooking.
- I have lost control of how much I use it. I find this stressful.
- It is stressful to have conflicts with my family who complain about my behavior.
- It is frustrating to get stuck in discussions on Facebook that do not lead anywhere.

I was able to identify as many advantages as disadvantages. Therefore, I chose digital balance as my main goal: to continue with social media but in a more controlled way.

I told my family and friends on Facebook about my detox and my goal. For the rest of the week, I would have at least three zones free from social media, places where I would normally use social media. I chose:

Breakfast: worked well

The bathroom: 2 relapses

Gym: went well

Travel by subway/bus: 2 relapses

Watching TV: 1 relapse

The relapses were undramatic. Suddenly I was back in my feed on Facebook and Jodel. But I did not feel guilty, instead I thought more practically about leaving my mobile in my pocket and just getting it out if I needed to check the calendar or other important things.

At home I chose to have the phone on charge in the kitchen and go out there if I needed to check something. I found myself stretching the limits with my zones. On the escalator on the subway, I pulled out my phone, and the gym surely didn't include the changing room? This way of thinking is typical of an addict. Trying to stretch the limits. Just like the alcoholic who always finds a reason to have a drink. And then one more.

At the end of the week, I became a moderator at Jodel. I was given the authority, in collaboration with others, to review reported posts. Being an online sheriff is a special responsibility. I have always thought it to be everyone's responsibility to combat racism, hatred, threats and sexism, therefore I usually report to the administrators if I think someone has crossed the line. But now I had the power to decide which posts would be left and which ones would be erased, an important task to keep the network reasonably free from stupidity. Since I was only in step 2 of the detox program, I accepted the mission.

On the last day of the week I went to the gym without my mobile. I left it on charge at home. It was a Sunday, so I didn't expect any work calls and I had no other need for it. I do not use any training apps and do not take photos at the gym. I have mostly used my phone to scan the feed on Facebook when using the exercise bike, and maybe post something in one of the groups that I am with.

Did I miss my phone? Not really. Earlier this week I had got used to not using social media. This was just another step down. I believe that my dependency is linked to social media and not to the mobile itself.

Step 3 – Look but don't act
During the third week, I would just look, not post, share, like or comment. The point of step 3 is to gradually get used to it. Being able

to look but not act is like a test of self-discipline. Like a smoker who goes into a tobacco store without buying anything. I also introduced the new routine of shutting down my mobile phone one hour before bedtime.

Monday: I am in a café writing a long post in an exercise group. But then I remembered. New phase. Just look – don't write. I had to delete my carefully worded text.

At the gym my routine worked well. No checking of my feed.

Now I suddenly posted a reply on Jodel. Get a grip Sven! How can it be so hard? Should I remove the apps? My idea was to challenge myself by having all the apps on my mobile. I removed notifications a long time ago. But is that enough? Yes, I think so. Now I just have to think for a moment every time I pick up my phone. Why am I doing it? And just do what I am supposed to do. If I check an email, I am finished when I have read and answered it. I do not need to scan any other feeds.

In the evening I sit on the couch at home with my mobile in my hand. I get an email from TripAdvisor telling me that I will soon reach a new level if I post a few more reviews.

So, I write a review about a nice café nearby. When my partner comes home, she wants to know what I'm doing. I explain and she wonders if that isn't the same thing as posting on social media. My answer is that TripAdvisor is not part of my detox. It is different to Facebook and Instagram. She sighs and believes this to be a classic defense. I do not agree. The next day I can admit she was right. I notice that I sometimes become restless and seek substitutes for the social media that I am avoiding. I need a change of plan. I'll include TripAdvisor in my detox. Or will I?

Tuesday: Today, there was a small challenge on Facebook. It was the birthday of a good friend and I normally congratulate my friends on Facebook. Especially those who are my "real" friends. But because of my detox, I couldn't. But since it was not a major birthday, I didn't really feel much pressure. I'll send a greeting afterwards.

Soon I will go down to the gym. I will bring my mobile with me but refrain from posting anything, just check the feed when I cycle. At the gym there was a mixed cardio training session and when I did my strength training I left my mobile to the side. But when I sat on the exercise bike, I checked my email and text messages.

I watched something interesting. There was a woman who was doing some strength training with her phone in hand. She alternated exercises with checking and writing something on her phone. She used the mobile more than the dumbbells. In the end she interrupted her training, writing eagerly with a big smile. Who knows, maybe she was going out for a nice lunch? I often see this phenomenon. That the mobile phone is not just a useful tool at the gym, but that selfies and social media take priority over the actual training. I notice a clear difference in focus if I am exercising without my mobile.

Late in the evening I watch a movie on my own. Just the cat and I on the couch. And the mobile.

Checked tomorrow's schedule and an email from a customer. Suddenly I find myself on Jodel. The mobile will have to stay in the kitchen from now on.

Wednesday: Today I have been careless. I took my mobile with me to the bathroom and immediately went onto Facebook. I will now try not to bring my mobile to the bathroom at all.

Thursday: I was about to travel on a train, but it was delayed. Normally, I would have expressed my frustration on social media. Now I messaged with my family instead. I think it can be one of the strengths of social media. To quickly and easily receive some empathy from a fellow human being. My substitute is now to bombard my family through our text group. It is unclear what the family thinks of this.

I just went over a small river. I often take a nice picture and post it. This time I just carried on by. I got an empty feeling. I am increasingly beginning to feel similarities with my nicotine addiction that I managed to break many years ago. Back then, I felt for a while that something was missing. A melancholy that was difficult to identify. For many years I had been used to lighting a cigarette in certain situations. Whilst having a coffee, when I was talking on the phone and strangely enough when I was out in the woods. The cigarette was a part of the experience. It should just be there. I feel the same now about my mobile and social media. Now that I have limited access, it feels a little boring, verging on sad. Like an important piece of my life has disappeared. This is proof that social media has fulfilled an important need. The difference to cigarettes is that I stopped smoking for good and the goal was to be smoke-free for the rest of my life. I hope to return to social media.

On the train home there were continued delays. I sent a new group message to my family and got some response. But was this silly? Using the family as a Facebook substitute. Or did it make sense? They are still my closest, my family. These are my thoughts as the train travels through the darkness of the countryside. Every other passenger has a screen in their hands, and they seem to have contact with their closest friends about the delay and their dinner plans. How did we manage before? We just accepted it. But hang on. Weren't there payphones on the trains? Well, during a period in the 80's, before the mobile boom, trains had a payphone onboard. So, it was possible to let people know about any delay. These are my thoughts go as go rolling home.

Friday: Today, there was continued spam messaging to the family. I sent pictures that they didn't really understand. In the end I called up my partner and talked for a while instead.

I had nice conversations with the guys at the gym. We were three authors in the changing room. We discussed social media and the internet. Ernst Brunner told us that he is now barely using email at all. For me, it feels both brave and strange. But on the other hand, we are in different phases of life. Ernst is older than I am and is less in the spotlight today.

An exciting reflection I have is that I have become more sociable since I stopped communicating through social media. I think I am talking more to people I meet in everyday life and that is perhaps better for my well-being in the long run.

Saturday: Today I have been close to breaking one of my free zones, the sofa. I sat half-way through the news when I realized that my fingers had moved towards the Facebook symbol on my mobile. It was meant to be in the kitchen. Get a grip, Sven.

When I went out with the cat there was no obligatory picture to post. How many people miss this? In all honesty, maybe I am the one who enjoys posting the pictures. Not my Facebook friends. Because they have already seen the cat lots of times. Sure, some animal lovers may like the picture. But there will be no barrage of likes.

In the evening I eat dinner with an old friend. Two middle-aged men are eating and talking for several hours. Neither of us check our mobile phones nor take a picture of the food. The conversation becomes more focused in that way. We talk about my detox project and whether I should go back to my previous life or not. Anders notes that he is not as bad as I am. He's right. Anders posts far less than I do.

Now it's only two days left. Detox starts on Monday morning. Quite exciting and scary. It was a long time since I was completely free of social media. I have been thinking about how strong this addiction is. Previously, I have seen it as a light risk-use. Like a bad habit that can be easily changed. Now I am starting to change my mind. It feels like a strong force, not to be ignored or made light of. But, as always, I think that everyone has the power to regain control. If the motivation is strong enough.

Sunday: A bit of work in the office. Exercised without social media and I picked up my partner at the train station.

Tomorrow is the big day. My total detox starts. I have mixed feelings about it. I am both curious and a little scared of how I will react. Posted a review on TripAdvisor from Saturday's restaurant visit. Will be pondering whether this is a substitute or not. The feedback is basically non-existent. Sometimes I get an email from TripAdvisor where they praise my posts. Apart from that, nothing much happens. I have no interaction with anyone else.

As I continue with my family texts, the responses become close to zero. I think they've seen through me.

Step 4 – A total detox

Now comes the biggest challenge of the program. During this week I will be completely free from all social media. This means that I will neither check, share, post, like nor comment. There is one exception. It is a Facebook group about children so addicted to their screens that they stay home from school. I started the group, and if there is an application for membership I have decided that I should go in and assess it. I don't think it will tempt me to stay on the phone.

Monday: I eat breakfast and then switch on my mobile. I see that something has happened in my Facebook group. I approved two new group requests. I think about whether to make my daughter an administrator.

I have decided to keep all the social media apps on my mobile. This makes it more of a challenge. Greater challenge and more training of my self-discipline. Just as I did when I was smoke-free for a while. Then I could challenge myself and sit close to someone else who was smoking. As a test of my willpower. It became a proof that I had defeated the nicotine addiction.

I go to the café where I normally have breakfast and I chat with the staff. Answer some messages. Most mornings I scan of my feed and am active on Facebook. What should I do now? TripAdvisor becomes the solution. I find that I have not reviewed the café I am in. So, I write a strong review. This is done quickly and then I have new work messages to reply to. On my way to a home visit, I slip onto Facebook. Leave quickly. It really is difficult to leave it alone. I check if my daughter can help approve new members in my Facebook group. Feel that it can be too great a temptation to start with something new. I change the settings so that all members can approve new ones. It feels better. A wise choice.

Tuesday–Thursday: I notice that I'm posting more and more on TripAdvisor and sending more texts to the family than ever. But when the response is weak, I give these substitutes up. Get an email from TripAdvisor where they praise me for my efforts and announce that I will soon reach another higher level. The absurdity is that, just as with likes on Facebook, it makes me happy. Silly really. When I go in and approve new members in my Facebook group, something happens. Suddenly I'm in another group. I'm starting to read the top posts and get caught up in one about screen time. I am eager to answer and think that it is relevant to my work. After a little thought

I decide to back off. I leave the group and try to think of something else. Yes! I managed to take control. This is exactly what I think is good with a liberal detox. To allow myself to get close to a relapse but then to regain control. I won over Mark Zuckerberg's algorithms. The battle is won – but not the war. Right now, it feels like a really tough challenge. Not as easy as I thought it would be.

Friday: I Today I go alone to the countryside to write, and now I only have the weekend left of my detox. It will be a challenge, because when I am in the countryside, I usually bombard Facebook with posts. I want to show everything that is beautiful, such as eagles and sunsets. When I am alone, it feels nice to have contact via social media. On the trip out, I download a chess app and play a few games. A nice pastime that is good for my brain and for keeping abstinence in check.

When I am out on the island, I take some pictures and film a little. I send some pictures to my family. But nothing is posted on Facebook. This feels good.

I call my elderly mother who has just been in hospital for heart problems. She feels well. Sending an email to Mark Griffiths in the UK. He is a researcher and specializes in various types of digital abuse. I explain that I am in the final stage of a detox and that is why I did not comment on his post on Facebook.

His answer was: 😊

I also see this behavior in others who do digital detox. That we somehow feel compelled to explain why we are detoxing. Instead of just doing it. We can see similar phenomena with alcohol. The person saying no, can feel forced to explain why. It shouldn't be like that.

Now, almost a whole day in the country has passed. It feels really relaxing. After supper I contact the family via text message. We send pictures of food and cats to each other. Like a compact Facebook. I'm curious about the discussion regarding screen addiction. With hesitation, I go in and check. But I do not comment. Defeat or victory? I think it's good that I don't comment. But I am a little disappointed with myself. Or am I? My basic idea was not to feel guilty if I didn't follow my plan exactly. Better to learn something from it and move on. Many people choose to remove the Facebook app to avoid the temptation. My method is more challenging.

Watch TV for a while and nod off in front of a chat show. I choose to have the phone switched on when I sleep, on silent. I want my family to be able to reach me. For landlines are a thing of the past.

Saturday: After a good night's sleep, I find that I have no messages. I can see that things happened on Instagram but choose not to check. At the end of my breakfast comes an email from a worried mother. Her son plays too much games and the mother asks for advice. I send a reply immediately.

After a writing session I go out to wash up. But since it is winter and icy outside, I always have my mobile with me. My nightmare is slipping and breaking my leg and not being able to call for help.

It is a different sort of feeling to do the washing up without posting on Facebook. I usually post a picture of the view and write something like: "with this view I don't mind doing the dishes". Just the kind of post that I used to ridicule before joining Facebook. I did not understand at all the point of sharing simple everyday events. I have changed that view. Think it is nice to be able to see and give insights into our everyday lives.

Now I notice how I become more aware of my surroundings. How the snow falls in fine flakes and a bird picking at my leftovers. Previously, Facebook was a filter for these things. It felt like Mark Zuckerberg ruled my experiences. Interestingly, I am increasingly beginning to mention his name. He seems to be a smart and creative person. I hope that I will have the opportunity to meet him sometime.

I'm in the final phase of my detox. The day after tomorrow I will make some important decisions. If and how to log in again. My goal has been to get more balance. Not to stop altogether. Now I am thinking about extending my detox. But I'm not sure. I start to think about how my Facebook friends see my absence. Before my detox I announced what was going on. Maybe that's why no one has been in touch. Or doesn't anyone care about my absence? My family and my closest friends have contact with me outside of Facebook. But everyone else? I will ask the next time I log in. Jodel then? How much do I miss it? At the time of writing, not at all. There is no Jodel in the archipelago. No activity at all and when I was in town, I didn't have any feelings of Jodel abstinence at all. It is an anonymous app and therefore it is easier to manage. Nobody knows who I am. No peer pressure as there can be on other platforms.

I have played a few chess games and think it is a rewarding pastime. I had contact with a client a few years ago whose father had a serious chess addiction. He had played away two marriages. I have taken the odd break by playing a game. The advantage of chess is that it is not particularly social. Even if you play against someone, the players are silent and focused on the game. You will not enter Facebook's eternal spiral of discussions, liking and sharing. It is a game that has a definite end. But I should make sure that it doesn't become too much, and that I stick to computer chess without real opponents. Otherwise, an opponent might pressurize me to keep playing. I had the same experience when playing games. Online games like WoW were easy to get into, while offline games were much easier to handle. A logical follow-up question will be whether I should try a total digital detox. Maybe over a weekend in the countryside. Worth thinking about.

Later in the evening I eat dinner and listen to Spotify. After my meal I send some pictures to my family and get some response! I'm not forgotten.

I'm looking at a Netflix movie. Drift off and go to bed.

Sunday: The last day of my detox. When I eat breakfast and look out over the bay, I have an inner calm that I have not known for a long time. I eat my yogurt and drink my coffee. Feel the flavors and enjoy the view. The difference is that I do not run out and take a photo to post. I often did that before breakfast. The subject could disappear. Unacceptable. I thought then. Now I take a photo after breakfast and let the picture sit in my mobile. It is much calmer for the mind. If I am honest, I realize that most of my pictures hardly revolution-ary. But that is the other side of the coin. To share simple everyday events. Even simple social interaction has its advantages. The ques-tion is whether it is possible to find a happy medium. As I maximize the benefits of social media while avoiding the disadvantages. That is what the next phase will be about. How to create a digital balance. Today I will go home and during the walk to the pier I experience an incredible peace. I enjoy the beautiful view. Without thinking "what a nice picture this will be on Facebook". It's soothing. I take some pictures, but they stay in my mobile.

On the boat to the mainland I play a few chess games.

"Look at that huge eagle", I hear someone say. I tear myself away from my mobile and look. A beautiful sea eagle glides just 50 meters from the boat. It seems to follow us. I go out on the deck to watch it. I take out my mobile and film it and take some photos. I talk to some other passengers who followed my example. When the eagle has disappeared from sight, I go back in and send the best picture to my family. No response.

Late in the evening I watch a movie on TV. The movie ends at 00.10. What do you think I'm doing next? Well, I check Facebook and

Jodel. I feel a strange sense of emptiness. Same pictures of skiing and cat clips as before my detox. But apart from that, mostly emptiness. Nothing has happened. I can observe the same reaction in gamers who return after a game break. "The magic is gone." But I don't post anything and go to bed according to plan.

Step 5 – Learn
Now I have arrived at step five. Now is the time to learn and decide how my life on social media is going to look.

When I told my partner that I had already looked into the world of Jodel, she was surprised and skeptical. We had a discussion that ended up in a minor argument. She thought that I should ease off with my mobile phone and not continue as I had before. She meant that I was just defending my addiction and that I didn't really want to change my behavior. When I let this sink in, I wondered if she was right. Have I just made a surface adjustment or is it the beginning of a real change?

During my detox I was able to stay away from Jodel, Instagram, Snapchat and LinkedIn. However, I took to Facebook a few times, but backed off when I realized that I was breaking my detox. It showed, as I had already suspected, that this was primarily a Facebook addiction.

I deliberately used TripAdvisor, chess and text messages to my family as a kind of substitute. However, I do not think I slipped into a new addiction. The kicks are significantly weaker when posting a review on TripAdvisor. I don't get the same instant feedback as on Facebook.

I was happy when I won at chess, but it didn't trigger me to play too much. It felt like a fun pastime that I had control over. My family texts didn't provide any response. I think my family got tired of my attempts at contacting them.

One positive experience was that I became more sociable. I am, basically, a very sociable person. But I noticed that I exchanged words with people I encountered in my everyday life more than usual, because my mobile was no longer in focus.

The digital stress of constantly updating and monitoring the feeds disappeared completely. Especially during my last detox days in the archipelago. I understood that I had a higher presence in my experiences. That I could observe and perceive things at a deeper level than before. It was true of everything from experiencing Mother Nature to enjoying food.

Micropauses
The first time I was restless. My habit of always filling out the small gaps with Jodel and Facebook came to the fore. I now had to handle the micropauses and I eventually found them to be relaxing. Being able to look out through a train window for a while, perhaps see a deer that I would otherwise have missed. Or just let your thoughts flow freely without digital distractions. My detox was perfect for me. I slowly but surely came attuned to another digital life – a life where I have the control.

My mobile addiction was cured
From the beginning, I felt that I mainly had a Facebook addiction. That the other aspects of my mobile use were under control and without problems. But afterwards I discovered that I had a tricky relationship with the mobile itself. That I sometimes picked it up and aimlessly clicked around among my apps. Not with any definite goal but as a strange habit.

That's why I was happy when I discovered a positive side effect of my social media detox – I no longer go around constantly with my mobile phone in my hand. In the past, it was like a natural extension of my arm. The mobile was always at hand, ready for service. Whether it was something necessary like using Google maps, or just checking something on Facebook. The mobile had become like a wristwatch, something was missing if it was not in place. But now I found myself walking across town with my phone resting in my pocket and I only took it out when I needed to check my seat on the train. A really nice feeling. I will continue with that. Only using the mobile when needed.

I have decided to test a mobile-free day-of-the-week. I will try it on Sundays. That will be my digital day of rest.

I will introduce some mobile-free zones as well: the bathroom, the sofa and the breakfast table. The difference with when I was on my detox is that, now, I am not just without social media, but I am also completely mobile-free. The advantage is obvious, because I am only logged on social media via my mobile. If I then limit my mobile usage it will also mean less Facebook.

My changes

I have become more economical with posts and comments. There is no need to post everything I experience, and I do not need to be involved in all discussions. If I experience a bad atmosphere in a group, I will choose to leave it. Life is too short for unnecessary discussions that do not lead anywhere.

I will focus my presence on social media on my work as a therapist, lecturer and author. The risk is that there will be fewer cat videos in my feed from here on.

An interesting question is whether I have considered logging out completely. Can a modern human sit outside of social media? Is it worth the price? Do I want to lose the benefits I see with social media? Not right now, anyway. I think that I want to settle for a digital balance. However, I will reduce my activity and take regular breaks.

Relapses

My motto when it comes to detox is not to have a bad conscience if you break your plan. A bad conscience often leads to feelings of guilt. Not having done what you should. It is rarely encouraging and can have the opposite effect. As you saw, I also had some minor relapses. But it encouraged me to try again. There is also a big difference if you take a short relapse or if you break a detox. In my case, they were just short blips, not a complete disaster.

My first steps back

Before I left home, I scanned through Instagram and Facebook. Snow-drifts in the mountains, fine dining and exercise. Just as before my detox, and nothing new at all. It is striking how little has happened during my absence.

During my morning visit to the coffee shop, I went in and commented on posts in my Facebook group. I posted my first Jodel in two weeks. I also submitted my first post on Facebook. There was no avalanche of likes. Bibbi welcomed me back and Sten wrote something philosophical about *event horizon*. I don't really know what I was expecting. Maybe applause about how good I had been, or curiosity about how I'd enjoyed it. I guess I'll just have to accept that it was not as big a deal as I thought it was. Or are people so busy and absorbed by Facebook that my actions might feel threatening? That I am actually challenging everyone's presence on social media.

Digital hangover

After a few days I realized that I had been less active than before my detox. I felt a distaste with posting too much, much like the feeling after eating and drinking too much during a party and then going back to normal. Besides my post at the beginning of the week on Facebook, I have just posted two things on Jodel. I have checked my other feeds and liked a few posts. How excellent it would be if my detox has worked! That was my goal. Being able to go back to being just a moderate user. But I'm wise enough to realize that this is only half the story. Now I have to go into situations where I used to bombard the social media sites with posts, so I must be self-disciplined and not slip into my old habits.

The other day I was interviewed by the Swedish daily newspaper, Aftonbladet, about my mobile addiction. The title was "Cures internet addiction – became addicted to his mobile". It describes very well what this is all about. How easily we can get hooked on something that is, in itself, positive, and that even an addiction expert can "fall down". I hope that with my knowledge, I can pave the way for greater openness about this kind of addiction.

In the evening I scrolled through my feeds and chose, sparingly, to like and comment. I saw a post about someone's mother dying. Is it reasonable to post this? Most likely, the person thought it helped and was a relief. But I don't know her. We are author colleagues. It still feels reasonable to offer my condolences. She likes my comment. I see that she is posting more and more pictures in memory of her dead mother. A natural part of the mourning process. I have seen similar phenomena during difficult divorces. How social media is used to communicate what has happened and to gain sympathy from friends. A natural and very human response to someone going through a crisis.

I travel to Uppsala for a home visit and lazily check my feeds. When I sit at my favorite café, the usual happens. I start talking to people I don't know. The thing we have in common is that everybody is a coffee nerd and, with an interest like that, it is difficult for Zuckerberg's algorithms to compete.

It strikes me that this was how it used to be. Strangers started chatting on a train or in a café. Today, our screens are an obstacle.

We don't even look up to greet people, our eyes are glued to a screen. But on the other hand, today's conversation shows that it is still possible to break through in the old-fashioned way.

Soon my detox will be finished. The last days on my 5-week program. Time has really gone quickly. When I started, it felt like a long time. Now it feels just perfect. Above all, I have had a lot of time to reflect. Now we'll see how it goes in practice.

Relapse

It's the first day after my 5-week detox program. Today I have primarily been active in connection with my profession. Privately, I have been very economical with my likes and not posted anything at all, just the odd comment on Jodel. My new focus on my professional activities feels great. It gives a greater sense of meaning to what I do.

I have just realized that I have three screens running at the same time. Writing on my lap top, the TV is on and the mobile phone is on the sofa. I immediately shut the TV off. Two screens are more than enough. We have coined an expression for this in the family: double screening.

After a few weeks I notice that I'm starting to slip on my routines. I have started taking my mobile with me to the bathroom, to the sofa and to the breakfast table. However, I have been diligent with my posting. I have also started some new groups. They focus on my work and I notice that I am increasingly using social media in support of my business. This is a tip that my wise daughter gave me a few years ago: "Put more energy into your work sites instead." As usual, my children are right.

Today I heard the brutal truth from my partner. She thought I had fallen back into old habits. That I had only switched my activity from my private Facebook account to my work platforms, and I always have the mobile in my hand. After defending myself, I realized she was right. Mark Zuckerberg's algorithms had me back in an iron grip. How can it be so difficult? I have taken a relapse. But had I really expected anything else? The advantage is that I can adjust my routines and find new tactics to win the match.

I agree that I lapsed somewhat on my mobile-free zones. I will take control of this and try to discipline myself. Because I preferred it when I had these zones. The same goes for the fact that I replaced my private Facebook with a professional profile. Is it okay or just a way to maintain my addiction? It feels more meaningful that I spend time on my business than watching cat videos, but I do not want it to make me a workaholic, and it is hard to know where to draw the line. For as an entrepreneur, I care very deeply about my business.

My conclusion is: Reintroduce mobile free zones. The bathroom, breakfast table, TV sofa and bedroom. I also have to set reasonable limits for my professional accounts. I should really delegate to my coworkers.

One month after my detox

Now it's been a month since my detox and it's time to evaluate. My presence on Jodel has felt completely okay. I will probably continue to Jodel at this basic level. I am worse with Facebook. Most of my mobile zones have again been invaded. I Facebook on the sofa whilst watching TV, in the bathroom and in the gym. Admittedly, I follow my plan to focus on my profession, but I notice that it sometimes gets too much.

I was recently up in the mountains. My plan was to be free from social media. It is a place where I am often triggered to post pictures of the wonderful mountain views. Therefore, it felt like a good challenge. Like not eating sweets during the Christmas holidays. Normally I would upload a picture early on in the trip and play the game "Where do you think I am going?" But this time I didn't, instead I read through this script. But what do you think happened halfway there? Well, a flock of reindeer blocked our way. We stopped the car and the beautiful animals passed over the road. I took some pictures with the mobile camera and intended to send them to my children. Five minutes later I had posted the best picture on Facebook. But I was supposed to be resting from Facebook during the week. So, that's how that went. I got some likes and some comments. Was it worth it?

But as usual, I had no bad feelings about my relapse. I was more surprised at how quickly it happened, without even a thought or a conscious decision. For the rest of the week, I chose to put up just a few pictures. I took lots of pictures but left most of them in my mobile. When I did post, I did it in the evening and not in real time. I was active in some professional groups and got stuck in discussions a few times. But I was still happy with my mountain week. I was much less active on Facebook than usual and my mountain experiences felt more vivid than ever. Again, an example of how social media can be like a disturbing filter which, when removed, makes us more present in the moment.

I have been more active on LinkedIn, completely according to my plan to focus on my professional life. The advantage is obvious. It feels meaningful not to get caught up in cat videos and endless discussions like I often do on Facebook. My next steps will be to re-establish my mobile-free zones. Once again...

How did it go then?

In recent weeks I have experienced something that I have not known for many years. I have been in the countryside in a lovely coastal environment. Fishing, sunsets, dinners with family and friends. All enjoyed more than ever. The reason was the break from social media. I didn't post anything. I didn't even feel tempted in the places where I would normally take a picture to post. The experience of the moment became stronger and I did not get distracted by the digital. Practically, I have eaten dinners with the mobile on charge and when I have been on the sea I have left the phone on land.

Do I then consider myself "cured" from my addiction? Yes, in the sense that I can now finally feel that it is me who is in control again. That my life on social media is not compulsive and routine. My experiences have meant that I make more conscious choices. That I try to think about how I use social media. That was also my goal with this journey. Achieving a digital balance.

The author's thanks

I would like to say a big thank you to:

Carl-Johan Forssén Ehrlin at Ehrlin Publishing who gave the thumbs up for this project, as well as for his quick and encouraging support through social media.

My fantastic editor Elin Ihreborn for her excellent cooperation and for being patient with all my thoughts and ideas.

My family who supported me through another book project.

Mark Zuckerberg for an invention that, when it works best, really brings people closer to one another.

My author colleagues at Author on Facebook.

All my friends on Facebook.

Everyone I interviewed, from students in playgrounds to researchers at universities.

I would like to extend my special thanks to Professor Mark Griffiths, Toni Prince Tvrtkovic, Elaine Eksvärd and Professor Fred Nyberg.

Sources and reading tips

Here you can read more about the different topics I have included in the book. I have obtained direct information from some sources and, from others, I have taken inspiration. Since research and studies are ongoing with regards to social media addiction, if you are curious, I recommend you search the internet for "Social media addiction" to find the latest findings.

Alter, Adam (2017) *Irresistible – The Rise of Addictive Technology and the Business of Keeping Us Hooked*, Penguin Press.
A description of the technology behind behavioral dependencies.

Bates, Sophie (2018). *A decade of data reveals that heavy multi-*

taskers have reduced memory, Stanford psychologist says. Taken from Stanford News. https://news.stanford.edu/2018/10/25/ decade-data-reveals-heavy-multitaskers-reduced-memory-psychologist-says/. Published 2019-10-25.
The risk of being disturbed in your feed.

Gelin, Martin & Pettersson, Karin (2018). *Internet är trasigt – Silicon Valley och demokratins kris*, Stockholm: Natur & Kultur.
Critical and in-depth examination of the major technology companies.

Helle, Siri (2019). *Smartare än din telefon – hur du använder mobilen för att må battre, bli effektivare och stärka dina relationer*, Stockholm: Natur & Kultur.
A personally written book about how the mobile may be used in a positive manner.

Hunt & Dong (2014). *Chinese city tests out sidewalk lanes for cellphone users.* Taken from CNN. https://edition.cnn.com/2014/09/15/world/asia/china-cellphone-sidewalk/index.html. Published 2014-09-16.
Pavements for mobile users.

Keen, Andrew (2016). *The Internet Is Not the Answer*, Grove Press
A critical book about the internet which still gives hope.

Lieberman, Matthew (2013). *Social – Why Our Brains Are Wired to Connect*, Broadway Books.
About the human as a social being.

Mack, Eric (2014). *City gets a 'No Cell Phones' walking lane, for now.* Taken from CNET. https://www.cnet.com/news/one-city-gets-a-no-cellphones-walking-lane-for-now/. Published 2014-07-18.
Pavements for mobile users.

Maushart, Susan (2011). *The Winter of Our Disconnect – How Three Totally Wired Teenagers (and a Mother Who Slept with Her iPhone) Pulled the Plug on Their Technology and Lived to Tell the Tale*, Penguin Putnam Inc.
A family's experiment of living without digital technology.

Nutley, Sissela (2019). *Distraherad – hjärnan, skärmen och krafterna bakom*, Stockholm: Natur & Kultur.
A deep-dive into how the brain is affected by our digital lives.

Reuters (2018). *Has the world gone mad? Mental health disorders on the rise globally.* Taken from France 24. https://www.france24.com/en/20181010-has-world-gone-mad-mental-health-disorders-rise-every-country-globally. Published 2018-10-10
Rising global mental ill-health.

Rollenhagen, Sven (2015). *Mobikett – handbok för mobilzombies*, Stockholm: Rollenhagens Forlag.
My own book with a focus on the rules and etiquette for mobile use.

Smith, Rory (2018). *France bans smartphones from schools.* Taken from CNN. https://edition.cnn.com/2018/07/31/europe/france-smart-phones-school-ban-intl/index.html. Published 2018-07-31
France's ban on mobile phones in schools.

Taplin, Jonathan (2017). *Move Fast and Break Things – How Facebook, Google and Amazon Have Cornered Culture and Undermined Democracy*, Pan Books.
A description of how some large IT companies dominate the business and do not take responsibility for their products.

Thoreau, Henry David (2006). *Walden*, Stockholm: Natur & Kultur (first published 1854, *Walden;or life in the woods*, Boston: Ticknor and Fields).

A timeless classic about how people have become more and more slaves to technology and risk losing out on the big questions in life.

TV-clip with Alicia Vikander, February 2018, Skavlan, SVT

Twenge, Jean M. (2018). *iGen – Why Today's Super-Connected Kids Are Growing Up Less Rebellious, More Tolerant, Less Happy– and Completely Unprepared for Adulthood–and What That Means for the Rest of Us,* Atria Books.
Fact-filled book about the online generation..

Wisterberg, Erik (2019). *Sverige tog precis ett rejalt kliv mot ett mobilförbud i skolorna.* Taken from Breakit. https://www.breakit. se/artikel/17835/sverige-tog-precis-ett-rejalt-kliv-mot-ett-mobil-forbud-i-skolorna. Published 2019-01-12.
Sweden's discussion about the ban of mobile phones in schools.

Zibreg, Christian (2018). *Facebook is testing Screen Time-like digital wellbeing features for its mobile app.* Taken from iDown-loadBlog. https://www.idownloadblog.com/2018/06/25/face-book-digital-wellbeing/. Published 2018-06-25.
Social responsibility amongst technology companies.

Interviews

Christina Bengtsson, focus expert. Interviewed via Messenger, September 2018.

Mark Griffiths, Professor in Behavioural Addiction. Interviewed in Stockholm, October 2018.

Karina Di Lucia, Digital Detox Center, Villa Insikt. Interviewed in Stockholm, September 2018.

Fred Nyberg, Professor in Biological Behavioural Research. Telephone interview, August 2018.

Elaine Eksvärd, expert in rethorics. Telephone interview, March 2018.

Toni Prince Tvrtkovic, Social Media personality. Interview in Stockholm, March 2018.

Valentin Oswald, Jodel. Email interview, June 2018.

Anton Fagerhem, John Severinson and **Lukasz Lindell**, Facebook. Interviews via email, Messenger and telephone. June 2018– February 2019.

Recommended links

Addiction Expert **Mark Griffith's** blog: https://drmarkgriffiths. wordpress.com/

Center for Humane Technology: https://humanetech.com/

For information about the different types of **diagnoses**: https:// www.psychiatry.org/psychiatrists/practice/dsm and https://icd. who.int/

Swedish organisation focusing on **NPF** (Autism, ADHD och such like): https://attention.se/varaprojekt/avslutade-projekt/natkoll/

Swedish branch of **Time Well Spent**: https://www.timewellspentsweden.com/

Statistics on **global internet usage**: https://datareportal.com/ reports/digital-2019-global-digital-overview